WESTWARD ON THE

BY THE EDITORS OF
AMERICAN HERITAGE
The Magazine of History

NARRATIVE BY
MARIAN T. PLACE

CONSULTANT
EARL POMEROY
*Beekman Professor of Northwestern and
Pacific History, University of Oregon*

PUBLISHED BY
**AMERICAN HERITAGE
PUBLISHING CO., INC.**
New York

BOOK TRADE DISTRIBUTION BY
MEREDITH PRESS

INSTITUTIONAL DISTRIBUTION BY
HARPER & BROTHERS

OREGON TRAIL

THE HUNTINGTON LIBRARY

FIRST EDITION
LIBRARY OF CONGRESS CATALOG CARD NUMBER: 62-17442
© 1962 by American Heritage Publishing Co., Inc., 551 Fifth Ave., New York 17, N. Y. All rights reserved under Berne and Pan-American Copyright Conventions. U. S. copyright is not claimed for color plates.

Foreword

Americans have moved westward to new homes since early in the seventeenth century, when they heard of better farmlands in the Connecticut Valley or up the James River. Before the Revolution they had adopted as their moving vans the Conestoga wagons of western Pennsylvania that we know as the covered wagons of novels and movies. Most Eastern states had their pioneer roads, now largely forgotten outside local histories. But the Oregon Trail, the first road to the Pacific slope, was the greatest of all the trails, and a wagon trip over it was one of the most memorable of American experiences.

The road to Oregon was a much longer and harder road than American pioneers had known before. The typical early settler in the Midwestern states who wanted a new farm found the frontier close enough to spy out the land before he occupied it; on the average, his children grew up only about three hundred miles away from their grandparents. But for the family that sought a new life west of the Missouri River in the early 1840's, there seemed to be no stopping place short of the Willamette Valley in the Oregon country. Settlers had to cross nearly 2,000 miles of plains, deserts, canyons, and mountains, so unfamiliar and inhospitable that to pause on the way was dangerous, to settle down unthinkable.

Eventually, some of the land along the Oregon Trail became habitable—after the Indians gave it up and Westerners tried irrigation and dry farming—and the gaps between outposts of civilization narrowed. Yet covered wagons and oxcarts still rolled to the Pacific Northwest even after tourists went by Pullman car to San Francisco.

The story of these pioneers pushing westward, which Mrs. Place retells here from their records, is the most authentic kind of romance. Their journey required not only toughness and courage, but also hope, imagination, and a vision of the future. It screened out the weak and those of little faith just as the transatlantic passage had tested the settlers of Puritan New England.

Recording the routine of life on the Trail, contemporary drawings and paintings also suggest the impact of the strange and sometimes forbidding landscape. Complementing these artists' impressions are photographs that capture so realistically the look of the hardy men and women seeking the Promised Land. In later years Northwesterners referred to the experiences of their ancestors on the Oregon Trail almost as the Israelites recalled their search for the land of Canaan. To have been a descendant of these pioneers was to claim a heritage that helped inspire and unify the people of a nation.

EARL POMEROY

A pioneer family, all its worldly goods stowed in its wagon, seeks a new life in Oregon.

Six new AMERICAN HERITAGE JUNIOR LIBRARY *books are published each year. Titles currently available are:*

WESTWARD ON THE OREGON TRAIL

THE FRENCH AND INDIAN WARS

GREAT DAYS OF THE CIRCUS

STEAMBOATS ON THE MISSISSIPPI

COWBOYS AND CATTLE COUNTRY

TEXAS AND THE WAR WITH MEXICO

THE PILGRIMS AND PLYMOUTH COLONY

THE CALIFORNIA GOLD RUSH

PIRATES OF THE SPANISH MAIN

TRAPPERS AND MOUNTAIN MEN

MEN OF SCIENCE AND INVENTION

NAVAL BATTLES AND HEROES

THOMAS JEFFERSON AND HIS WORLD

DISCOVERERS OF THE NEW WORLD

RAILROADS IN THE DAYS OF STEAM

INDIANS OF THE PLAINS

THE STORY OF YANKEE WHALING

GILCREASE INSTITUTE

Contents

1.	THE WAY WEST	10
2.	THE TRACKLESS LAND	24
3.	TRAPPERS' FRONTIER	34
4.	WAGONS OVER THE MOUNTAINS	46
5.	MISSIONARIES TO THE HEATHEN	56
6.	A HIGHWAY OF DESTINY	72
7.	THE GREAT EMIGRATION	84
8.	FRONTIER ON THE PACIFIC	96
9.	THE MORMON TREK	108
10.	THE RUSH FOR GOLD	118
11.	END OF THE TRAIL	134
	ACKNOWLEDGMENTS	149
	FOR FURTHER READING	149
	INDEX	150

ILLUSTRATED WITH PAINTINGS, PRINTS, DRAWINGS, AND PHOTOGRAPHS OF THE PERIOD

COVER: *A long wagon train bound for Oregon snakes its way upward into the foothills of the Rockies.*
COLLECTION OF C. R. SMITH

FRONT ENDSHEET: *Alfred Jacob Miller painted this fur-trading caravan crossing the prairies in 1837.*
BOATMEN'S NATIONAL BANK OF ST. LOUIS

BACK ENDSHEET: *The howling fury and sudden death of an Indian raid fills Charles Wimar's 1854 canvas.*
MUSEUM OF ART, UNIVERSITY OF MICHIGAN

The small wagon train in this 1850 painting plods across the vastness of the great plains on its long, tortuous way west. The Oregon Trail was a strange and frightening adventure for the pioneers, many of whom were completely unprepared for the hardships they had to face.

COLLECTION OF MR. AND MRS. JOHN F. MERRIAM

1.
The Way West

A festive air enlivened the covered wagon encampment near Independence, Missouri, on the morning of May 22, 1843. The prairie schooners, bright with fresh paint and white canvas tops, sparkled in the spring sunshine. While the menfolk pinned the yokes to the ox teams, the women snuffed out the cookfires. Children and dogs raced about, scattering chickens, jumping over churns and wagon tongues, and playing hide-and-seek behind the huge wheels. All seemed confusion until a man's voice rang out above the racket: "Turn out, turn out!"

A great cheer burst forth. "Oregon or bust!" the men shouted in answer. Some fired their guns skyward in sheer exuberance. Others hastily stowed the remaining belongings in the wagons. Women climbed onto the high seats and reached for toddlers handed up to them. Older children scrambled up behind their parents or jostled for positions at the rear to peer out through the puckered opening in the canvas.

The guide waved his hat and pointed westward toward Oregon, the Promised Land. As the teams on the lead wagons laid into their yokes, the great iron-tired wheels rolled slowly forward. One after another the wagons moved out onto an ocean of green prairie. The great adventure began in sunshine and song. It ended 2,000 miles and five months later, as the weary travelers dragged to a halt on the banks of the great Columbia River.

From Missouri to Oregon this advance train of the great migration of 1843, and scores of caravans in the flood tide of settlement to follow, rolled over a well-worn trail. Landmarks named by grizzled trappers and campgrounds of earlier road makers were their guideposts. None except the scouts — called pilots then — knew anything about the trip; none could predict what one emigrant called "the ten thousand little vexations" of covered wagon travel.

For the children and the younger people, the journey was a long, exciting picnic; for some of the ailing and the elderly, it meant a trailside grave; for farmers, merchants, and crafty adventurers, the exhausting labor, the suffering, and the danger seemed worth the risk if, in the end, they all prospered.

The travelers would see prairies, deserts, mountains, and Indians like none they had ever seen along the Mississippi or eastward. They would savor the wild taste of antelope and buffalo meat; cower under cannonading thunder-and-lightning storms; stand off buffalo stampedes; and exclaim over bold sunsets and acres of wild flowers. They would throw snowballs in August; sing, dance, and pray around crackling bonfires; and pit their ordinary strength and courage against the harsh land and fearful weather.

Geography dictated the route of the Oregon Trail, and the geography of the West included nearly every sort of terrain imaginable. At its beginning the Trail was easy enough going. From the jumping-off places on the Missouri River, it angled off to the northwest,

KNOEDLER GALLERIES

Emigrant parties fording the Platte and other shallow plains rivers always had to watch for quicksand; it was particularly dangerous for their heavy, short-legged oxen. Alfred Jacob Miller made this sketch of a horse and rider struggling through a bed of quicksand in 1837.

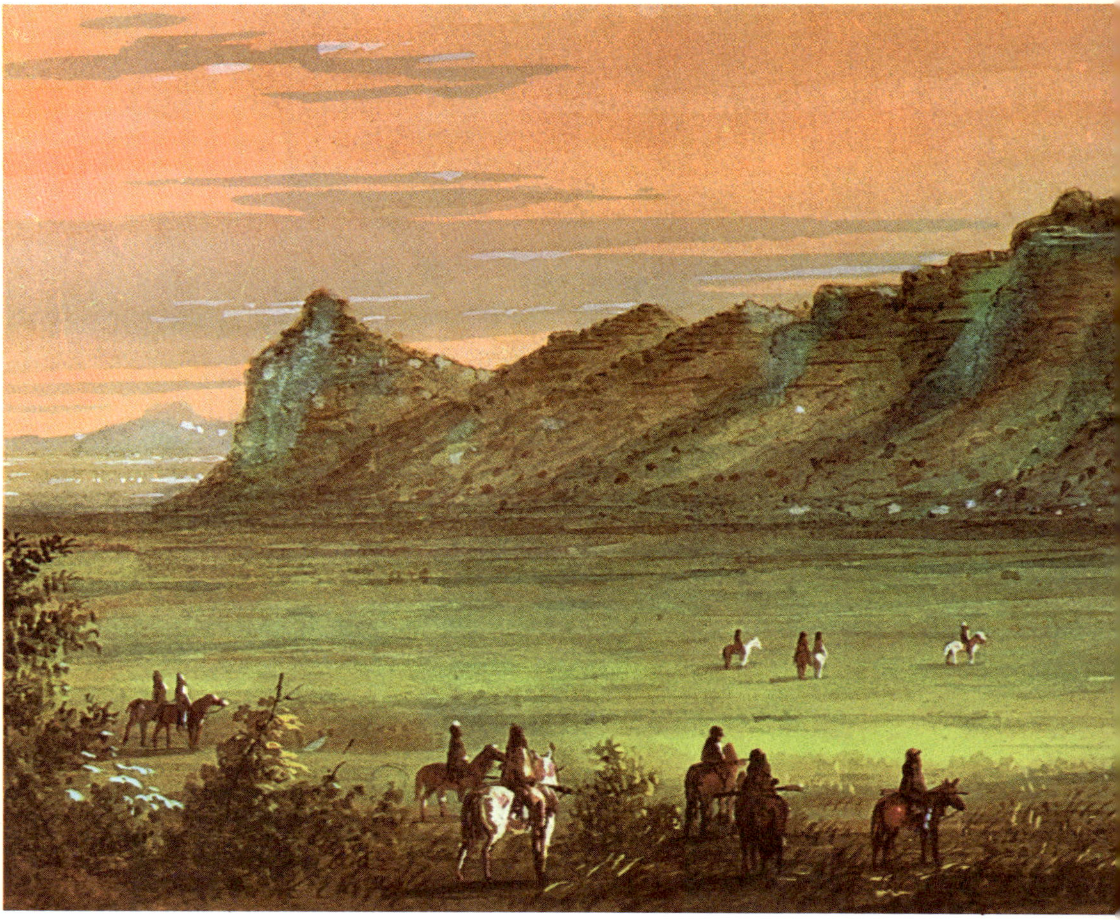

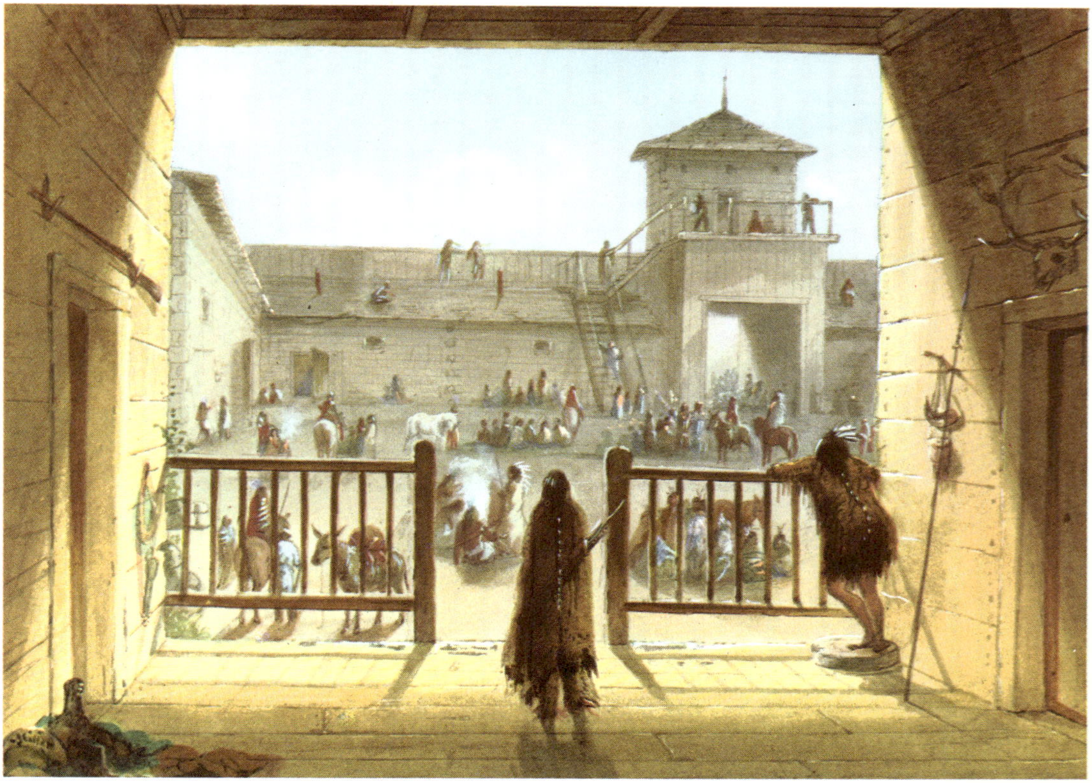

When the Scottish nobleman William Drummond Stewart went west in 1837, he employed a young Baltimore painter named Alfred Jacob Miller to make a pictorial record of the journey. Miller was the first to picture many of the great landmarks on the Oregon Trail, including Scotts Bluff (above) and Chimney Rock (right). His view of Fort Laramie at left shows Indians and trappers within the stockade.

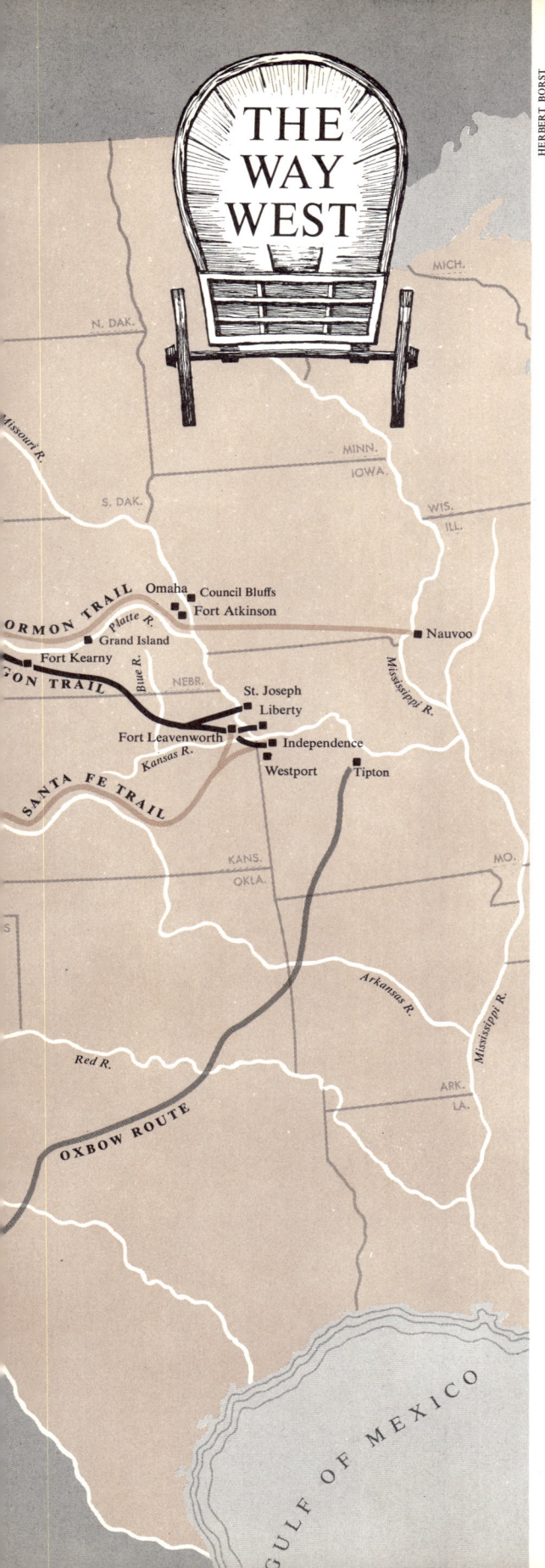

HERBERT BORST

This map traces the major trails west followed by trappers, explorers, and settlers before the coming of the railroads. The Oregon Trail was, from the very beginning of the wagon-train era in the 1830's, the most important of the overland routes; it was also the longest wagon trail in history, stretching some 2,000 miles through plains and mountains and deserts. The names of the landmarks on the Trail and of the forts eventually built along the way became part of American folklore while the Trail was still in use. Although many pioneers and adventurers used the Santa Fe, the Mormon, the California, and the Old Spanish trails, and later the "Oxbow" stagecoach route, it was along the Oregon Trail that the mainstreams of westward expansion flowed. The trails and alternate routes are shown as they were when they were first put to use. As the trails became more heavily traveled, they varied from their original courses by many miles because of the pressing need of the wagon trains for fresh water, firewood, and grazing land.

17

crossing the Kansas River and following its tributary, the Blue, to the valley of the Platte River.

From the line of bluffs called the "coasts of Nebraska" could be seen a level, grassy valley twenty miles wide, divided by the wide, shallow, lazily-flowing Platte. The bottom land was scarred with narrow paths worn by thousands upon thousands of buffalo moving to water. There were no trees.

After the forks of the Platte were reached, the road became more difficult. The crossing of the South Platte, swift-flowing and treacherous with quicksand, brought tragedy to many a party. The Trail followed the North Platte, the distant dunes broken by jutting, fragmented formations. Court House Rock, Chimney Rock, and Scotts Bluff were as much signposts as Main Street or Elm Street back east.

Fort Laramie, in southeastern Wyoming, was the first way station on the Trail, where emigrants rested and exclaimed over snow-capped Laramie Peak bristling up on the horizon. Here they could pick up news of the Trail ahead and enjoy, as one traveler described it, the welcome pleasures of "a room upstairs which look verry mutch like a bar room of an eastern hotel."

Moving steadily upward into the foothills of the Rockies, the Trail left the North Platte and followed the Sweetwater River. The bulky turtle-back of Independence Rock, one of the most famous landmarks of the Trail, loomed up, to be followed by a forbidding gorge known as Devil's Gate.

Days of steady pulling up the Sweetwater's banks brought the trains to the crest of the Continental Divide and South Pass, the summit gateway for wagons crossing the Rocky Mountains. Beyond, the rivers flowed to the Pacific.

As important as it was, South Pass was not the dramatic, spectacular cut through towering peaks that most of the emigrants had imagined. One of them complained that "If you dident now it was the mountain [pass] you woldent now it from aney other place."

The way was downhill now, but no less difficult. The Little Sandy and the Big Sandy rivers led to the beautiful Green River Valley. This had once been the heart of the beaver country, but by the time wagons rolled to Oregon, it was almost trapped out.

The Trail turned northwest into present-day Idaho. At Soda Springs, children spilled from the wagons and drank effervescing water that tickled their noses. Nearby Steamboat Springs, they discovered, really did sound like the steamboats that chuffed up the Missouri and Mississippi and Ohio rivers "back home." Here the road angled sharply to the north, across a hot, dry, sagebrush-covered plain. Drooping spirits brightened once the whitewashed walls of Fort Hall came into sight on the Snake River. The fort provided another welcome touch of

This 1883 painting shows an Indian war party watching a wagon train passing through its territory. The danger of Indian attack kept guards and scouts ever on the alert.

COLLECTION OF C. R. SMITH

The trappers on horseback in the corner of this striking Miller painting seem small and insignificant amidst the wild beauty of the Wind River Mountains.

civilization, no matter how primitive.

California as well as Oregon was held to be a Promised Land, and near Fort Hall those taking the California Trail turned southwest. They had scorching deserts and the snow-covered ramparts of the Sierra Nevada range to face before reaching their goal. Those bound for Oregon continued northward, their next stop Fort Boise.

The Trail wound through the Snake River country, a rocky, sandy, parched landscape that seemed to belong more on the moon than on the earth. After Fort Boise the Idaho Mountains closed in, with snow powdering the higher slopes and threatening lagging parties with the horrors of being marooned for the winter. The final barrier was the Blue Mountains, a trial for exhausted men and animals. At last came Fort Walla Walla and the Columbia River. Here was the Promised Land.

The last leg of the journey was made by boat, from either Fort Walla Walla or The Dalles, a series of rapids in the Columbia. South of the Columbia and up the Willamette their long trek ended. In the lush Willamette Valley they felled trees and raised their cabins, and their plows bit deeply into the soil.

The majority of the emigrant parties had a relatively safe passage when compared to the dangers and hardships experienced by those whose moccasins or horses had marked out the Oregon Trail. The long, ponderous caravans had maps and wheel ruts to guide them and wilderness forts to ease their needs. Most had men and guns enough to stand off Indians and build roads. All these advantages had been wrought for them at great cost in human life and suffering.

Yet, even though the Trail had been broken and marked, it was never an easy decision for a man to load his wife and children and all his belongings into a wagon and set out across endless miles of raw and untamed wilderness. It was a hard and unforgiving land they had to cross, and the cost was high. It has been estimated that in the pioneering years the trail west took the lives of some 34,000 people — seventeen for every mile.

A man who went west in 1843 wrote this of his fellow emigrants: "They have undertaken to perform, with slow moving oxen, a journey of two thousand miles. The way lies over trackless wastes, wide and deep rivers, rugged and lofty mountains, and is beset with hostile savages. Yet . . . they are always found ready and equal to the occasion, and always conquerors. May we not call them men of destiny?"

The Oregon Trail was more than just a pioneer road between Independence in Missouri and Fort Walla Walla in the Oregon country. It was the saga of westering Americans seeking ever more new land, a vital part of the national anthem that sang the story of the colonization of America. "Eastward I go only by force, but westward I go free," wrote Henry David Thoreau. "This is the prevailing tendency of my countrymen. I must walk toward Oregon. . . ."

YALE UNIVERSITY LIBRARY

Shown here is a turbulent, dangerous stretch of rapids in the Columbia River known as The Dalles, drawn by a British army officer in the 1840's. This narrow chute was the last major hazard faced by the pioneers seeking a new and better life in the fertile Oregon country.

The prairies of the West were once the home of uncounted millions of buffalo. Generations of Indians relied on the shaggy beasts for food and clothing, as did the first pioneers who moved west. Later, white men slaughtered the buffalo almost to the point of extinction.

DENVER ART MUSEUM

2.
The Trackless Land

Ages past, the restless land quieted from mountain building. Ancient seas withdrew and glaciers waned. The mammoth, the rhinoceros, the saber-toothed tiger, and the dinosaur no longer roamed over what is now the western half of the United States. There were no tracks on the land.

But life burgeoned anew. Southward across the land bridge then connecting Siberia and Alaska moved the ancestors of today's western wildlife: deer, elk, buffalo, the gray wolf and beaver, even the grizzly bear. The pronghorn antelope emerged, the only hoofed mammal native to the continent.

When man finally appeared, he followed these game trails southward to a sunnier, open grassland. He sought low passes over the mountains to reach the great plains. The earliest red man touched the land as lightly as did the smoke from his campfires. His descendants left few permanent traces, other than spearheads and medicine rings, as they ranged widely to hunt or wage war. Their greatest enemy was the land itself, generous and stingy in turn, with extremes in weather and immense distances.

The red men of the West mostly sought the buffalo, source of their food, clothing, tools, excitement, and old-man's tales. The shaggy creature had multiplied into the millions. Its hooves cut deep furrows in the plains, and its yellow teeth devoured the thick grass. It fouled the sweet water but fertilized the land. Spring after spring the grass greened, and Indians and wildlife gained a sturdier hold on their wilderness home. Then white men crossed the Mississippi River.

Eastward the white man's boots and wagon tracks had crosshatched the wilderness, welding scattered colonies into a fledgling nation. But the westering had halted at the near shore of the broad, brown Mississippi. The far wooded shore was sanctuary to deer, wild turkeys, and bright parakeets.

It was also alien land, yoked first to France, then to Spain, and then, in 1800, to France again. President Thomas Jefferson worried about the threat of a foreign neighbor so close. After highly secret conferences in 1803, he purchased from France what was called the Louisiana Territory.

"How large is this territory? How far does it extend?" the American emissaries questioned the negotiator, Talleyrand. The wily Frenchman answered truthfully, "I do not know." It really did not matter. By acquiring Louisiana the young nation had doubled its size.

Even before the Louisiana Purchase, Jefferson had been deeply interested

In 1792 Yankee sea captain Robert Gray (right) helped lay America's claim to the Oregon country by sailing up a river that he named the Columbia, after his ship. The Lewis and Clark expedition strengthened that claim when it marched overland to the mouth of the Columbia in 1805. The woodcut below shows Lewis (left) and Clark powwowing with Indians during their trip.

OREGON HISTORICAL SOCIETY

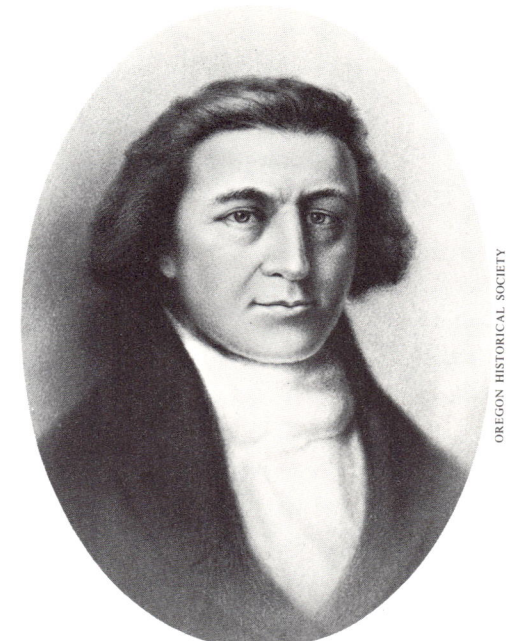

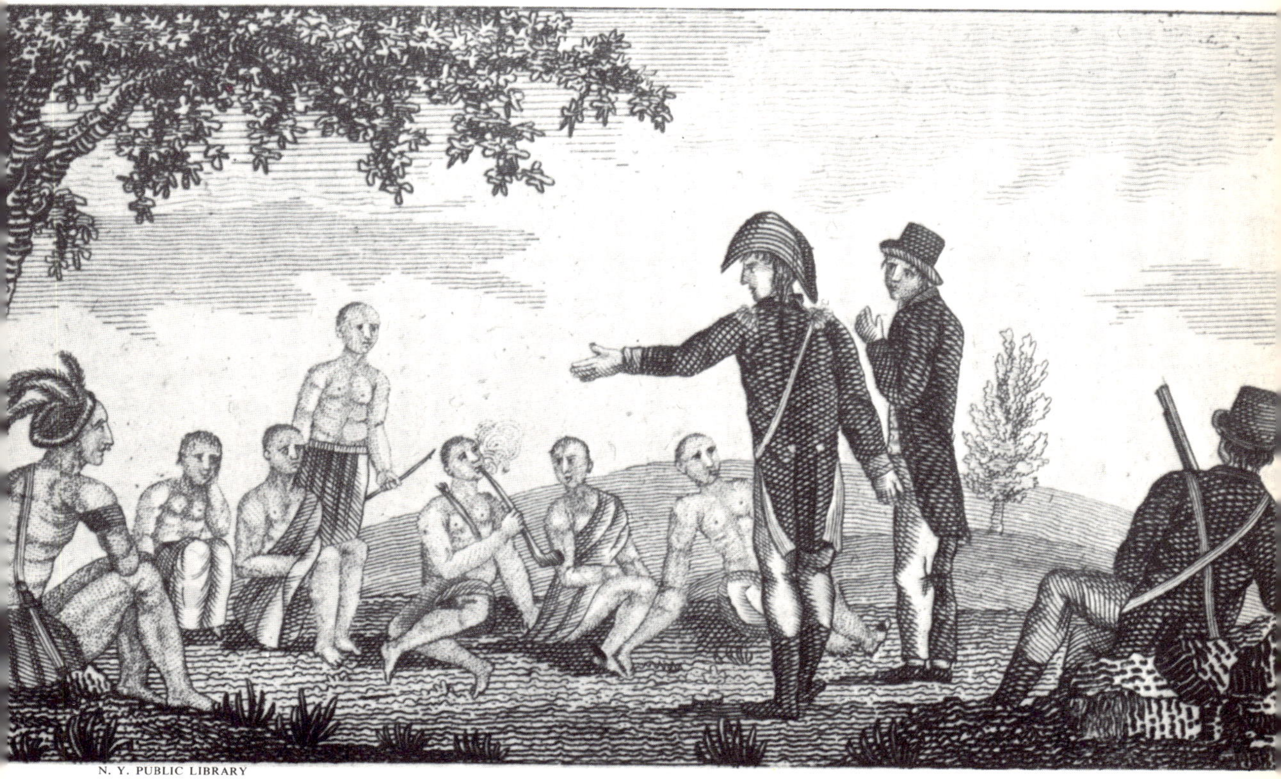

N. Y. PUBLIC LIBRARY

in investigating the nearly 830,000 square miles of this unmapped wilderness. He had asked Congress to authorize an expedition "To explore the Missouri River, & such principal streams of it, as, by its course & communication with the waters of the Pacific Ocean, may offer the most direct & practicable communication across this continent, for the purposes of commerce." Now there was the added need to bolster by exploration America's hold on this vast land.

A Corps of Discovery—forty-three men captained by Meriwether Lewis and William Clark—left St. Louis on May 14, 1804. It fulfilled its purpose, ascending the Missouri River beyond its great falls, crossing the Continental Divide, and descending the mighty Columbia River to the Pacific Ocean.

Lewis and Clark were not the first white men to see the Columbia rushing seaward to be swallowed in foaming ocean breakers. As early as 1741 Russians were trapping thousands of sea otter along the coast and shipping them to China. Surely they saw evidence of this great river pouring into the ocean. Captain George Vancouver of Great Britain explored the coastline fourteen years later. In 1778 another Britisher, Captain James Cook, traded a fortune in furs from the Indians of the coastal inlets nearby.

However, not until May 11, 1792, did anyone actually explore the Columbia. Only sixteen years after the birth of the United States, a Boston sea captain named Robert Gray entered the six-mile-wide mouth and anchored safely upstream. He named his discovery after his ship, the *Columbia*, and thereby laid a foundation for later American claims to the region.

Jonathan Carver, whose *Travels Through the Interior Parts of North America* was published in 1778, had referred to "the River Oregon, or the River of the West, that falls into the Pacific Ocean." But Carver's "River of the West" was pure myth, and where the word "Oregon" (or "Ouragon," as it was sometimes spelled) comes from is a mystery to this day. Nevertheless, the surrounding region, between the Rocky Mountains and the Pacific Ocean, and between British America on the north and Spanish America on the south, gradually came to be known as the Oregon country.

Lewis and Clark's Corps of Discovery retraced its path homeward, arriving at St. Louis on September 23, 1806. The men brought back glowing reports of astounding natural resources, great plains and barrier peaks, hostile and friendly Indians, a puzzling profusion and scarcity of game, and an abundance of beaver and otter. Since an edition of their journals was not published until 1814, the story passed by word of mouth. The lure that drew men across the Mississippi and up the Missouri was not land, or grass, or timber. It was beaver.

Hearts pounded, eyes glistened, and pulses quickened at the prospect of the fortune awaiting whoever made a rich haul of the prized, paddle-tailed ro-

John Jacob Astor was already the greatest name in the American fur trade when, in 1810, he set out to create a mighty fur empire in the Oregon country.

dent. For decades British and French Canadians had trapped one watershed after another west from Hudson Bay to the Pacific. Thanks to Alexander Mackenzie, who was first across the continent and reached the Pacific on July 20, 1793, Great Britain had a firm claim to what was to become Canada. Now Hudson's Bay Company fur brigades and posts, and those of the rival North West Company, were appearing on the tributaries and upper waters of the Snake and Missouri rivers. This was claimed as American territory, thanks to Lewis and Clark. Public sentiment developed for ousting the British "interlopers."

Little was said of distant Oregon, and seemingly only one man had Oregon on his mind. He was John Jacob Astor, a German-born immigrant grown wealthy from trading in Great Lakes pelts. Talk of prime mountain-country beaver excited him. He dreamed of a monopoly that would capture both the inland beaver and marten trade and the Pacific coast sea otter commerce. Organizing the Pacific Fur Company, he dispatched two expeditions, one by land and one by sea, to establish a headquarters at the mouth of the Columbia.

The seabound expedition left New York harbor on the *Tonquin* in September, 1810. On reaching its destination the crew built a small log post and,

FANNING, *Voyage to the South Seas*, 1838

OREGON HISTORICAL SOCIETY

An Astor party completed the rude trading post of Astoria at the mouth of the Columbia, on the site shown above, in 1811. They had arrived aboard the Tonquin *hoping to open a Pacific fur trade with China.*

As Astoria was being built, the Tonquin sailed north to trade. Indians attacked the ship (left) off Vancouver Island. A wounded crewman set off the powder magazine, blowing the ship and all aboard sky-high.

not surprisingly, called it Astoria. But soon after, an Indian attack and the explosion of her powder magazine put an end to the *Tonquin* and all aboard.

The land expedition, under the leadership of Wilson Price Hunt, left St. Louis in March, 1811. The original plan was to follow the route of Lewis and Clark. But in present-day South Dakota, Hunt heard harrowing tales of Blackfoot savagery inflicted on those foolish enough to continue up the muddy, winding Missouri. So, turning due west, Hunt led his men on a tough course over plains and mountains to the Snake River. Here they abandoned their horses for crude dugouts and unknowingly hurtled into some of the wildest water and deepest canyons on the continent. After terrible suffering, they arrived at Astoria.

The situation was desperate. The fur post was to have been supplied from New York, but now that the *Tonquin* was lost, how could the men stranded in the wilderness make their needs known?

The partner-in-charge at Astoria, Duncan McDougall, ordered a party of seven to carry dispatches overland from the Pacific to New York. The leader of this history-making brigade was Robert Stuart, who had come on the *Tonquin* and luckily remained at the stockade when the vessel sailed northward to its doom. Hardy, even-tempered, and resourceful, the twenty-seven-year-old Scotsman was an ideal choice for the dangerous assignment.

Stuart kept a detailed journal, *The Return from the Mouth of the Columbia to the Missouri.* Although he described vividly the fantastically big trees, rich soil, wildlife, and Indians of the lower Columbia, he viewed these as a businessman, not as a poet or naturalist. He noted beaver prospects, but never mentioned the staggering impact of high peaks and limitless plains on a man's soul. Nevertheless, the account is exciting reading; in unexaggerated prose it furnishes the details of the first blazing of the Oregon Trail.

Stuart began optimistically: "In the afternoon of Monday the 29th June 1812, 23 sailed from Astoria, under a salute of cannon from the Fort." His men paddled canoes made of quarter-inch-thick cedar, braced by boards secured with sturgeon twine and caulked with gum. On July 31, the Astorians turned away from the great Columbia. They transferred their "packages" of trade goods, ammunition, records, and personal belongings to fifteen horses obtained from Indians and steered a south-southeast course into hilly country. Forty-five waterless miles taught them the harsh discomfort of thirst.

In spite of maddening mosquitoes and sultry heat that drained their strength, the Astorians doggedly pressed southeastward through present-day Idaho. By early September the weather was becoming disagreeably cold. Friendly Shoshone Indians provided dog meat, dried salmon, and a flavorsome cake made of ground roots and serviceberries. Up to this time Stuart and his men had followed water courses. Now they sought "the Indian Road"—the land trail.

Early one morning Stuart heard the horses being stampeded. "To arms! Indians!" he shouted. But by the time his men stumbled from their blankets, Crows had run off all their horses. Being afoot in mountain country, with the cold breath of approaching winter frosting their blankets, was enough to make strong men lose heart, but they shouldered packs and trudged on. On October 22, 1812, a broad spur of mountains (in western Wyoming) blocked their way. To the weary, half-starved men it seemed impassable. But Stuart persevered until he found a low, open pass across these Wind River Mountains. Although he did not appreciate what he had done, he had found a mountain pass which horses and wagons could surmount. He had located South Pass, the gateway through which a westward migration could move on wheels from St. Louis to the Pacific. Looking eastward from the summit, he wrote, "Ahead the country in every direction south of east is a plain, bounded only by the horizon."

Stuart made his way to the Sweetwater River and then to the North Platte. Here he located a fording and a route to the Missouri River. On Friday, March 30, 1813, "We a little before sun set reached the Town of St. Louis, all in the most perfect health, after a voyage of ten months from Astoria."

The Oregon Trail was blazed.

Robert Stuart, who lived until 1848, saw the overland route he blazed become the great Oregon Trail.

Hotly pursued by Indians, the trappers in this 1850 painting are fleeing for their lives. These mountain men were an incredibly tough breed, who lived by their wits in the wilderness, facing every sort of hazard from savage Indians to ferocious grizzly bears.

COLLECTION OF BRONSON TREVOR

3.
Trappers' Frontier

There was no rush to settle on the newly acquired land between St. Louis and the Oregon country. One reason was a widespread belief that much of that land was a desert.

In 1806 Lieutenant Zebulon M. Pike explored the central portion of the Louisiana Purchase. After traveling across Kansas to Colorado, he reported that this superb grazing land was akin to "the sandy deserts of Africa." He advised his countrymen to "leave the prairies, incapable of cultivation, to the wandering and uncivilized aborigines." To ordinary folk the word "prairie" meant a place without trees, thus having poor soil.

In 1819 Major Stephen H. Long, of the U.S. Army Corps of Engineers, led a small party of soldiers, adventurers, and scientists across the central plains. His report was the first to call the interior a "great American desert." Long decided that the desert could be of great importance if it served as "a barrier to prevent too great an extension of our population westward."

After that, map makers and writers of schoolbooks labeled the vast stretch between the Mississippi and the Rockies as The Great American Desert, and this picture became entrenched firmly in the public mind. As far as most people knew, the desert and mountains

A friendly group of Kiowa Indians visits a camp on the Platte River set up by Major Stephen Long on his 1819-1820 exploration of the central plains. This water color was done by Samuel Seymour, the expedition's official artist.

were impassable and the only way to Oregon was by boat around South America and up the Pacific coast to the Columbia River. Thus, for a while, the through-trail which the Astorians had blazed was forgotten.

But on February 13, 1822, in the St. Louis *Missouri Gazette & Public Advertiser*, there appeared an advertisement that opened a new chapter in American history. General William H. Ashley sought one hundred young men "to ascend the river Missouri to its source, there to be employed one, two, or three years." Ashley and his partner, Andrew Henry, planned to dispatch parties of mountain men to the untrapped interior Rockies where beaver-dammed streams flowed down from tangled peaks.

One of Ashley's new recruits was a tall, brown-haired, twenty-three-year-old American named Jedediah Smith. He was a fair hunter even then, who neither smoked, chewed tobacco, swore, nor drank intoxicating spirits. Wherever he traveled, he carried a Bible. His companions numbered other future greats of the Oregon Trail—Jim Bridger, James Clyman, and Thomas Fitzpatrick.

After one winter trapping on the upper Missouri, Smith advanced to the position of expedition leader. In Sep-

While no true likeness of Jedediah Smith exists, artist Harvey Dunn has succeeded in capturing something of the indomitable spirit of this famous trapper and explorer.

tember, 1823, Ashley outfitted Smith, Fitzpatrick, Clyman, and some eight others at Fort Kiowa, near what is now Chamberlain, South Dakota. Smith led them westward up the White River, through the Black Hills, and into the remote Powder River country. Here, in a thicket, Smith came face to face with a grizzly bear. The bear gripped Smith's head between its jaws and clawed him terribly. Although badly injured, Smith told Clyman to sew up his wounds. One ear was nearly ripped off. Clyman did his clumsy best, and within ten days Smith was riding again. His face was scarred, and one eyebrow was askew, but his long hair covered the mangled ear.

Slowly, against icy winds, they rode westward to the Crow winter camp. This was in a sheltered valley at the foot of the east slope of the Wind River Mountains. The Crows were friendly, and their tepees were warm. For tobacco and trinkets, they swapped mountain beaver pelts far superior to Missouri River skins, being bigger, longer-haired, and silkier. Through garbled talk and sign language, Smith tried to learn if more such beaver were in the mountains beyond.

Yes, the Crows indicated, many beaver. The trappers were excited and sought more information. Since the Wind River peaks could not be scaled, how could they get around them? Was there a low pass? Smith had difficulty making the Crows understand what he wanted to know. Finally Clyman covered a buffalo robe with sand and scooped up several piles to represent mountains. Then he "walked" two fingers up and down.

The Crow chief nodded, and he rearranged the mountains, traced rivers in the sand, and leveled a low place between two of the peaks. The white men took careful note. In late February, 1824, they started out on ponies. Through deep snow and screaming winds they struggled along the south branch of the Wind River, topped a ridge, and came down on the Sweetwater River. A howling blizzard nearly finished them, yet they managed to make camp in a sheltered valley. They subsisted largely on mountain sheep.

In the second week of March, hunger made them set out again. They followed the Sweetwater upriver. Mountains loomed to the north and south as Smith led the way up and across a long, gradual, twenty-mile-wide slope scoured free of snow. On the far side, when he broke the ice in Big Sandy Creek, he discovered that the water flowed westward. His party had crossed the Continental Divide.

Smith, Fitzpatrick, and Clyman were the first Americans to cross this 7,550-foot-high pass from east to west. And this time the "Southern Pass," or South Pass, first used by the Astorians, was not forgotten.

Smith dispatched Fitzpatrick, Clyman, and others to deliver the furs via the Sweetwater, Platte, and Missouri route to Ashley, in St. Louis. Meanwhile, Smith and a few men trapped westward toward the Grand Tetons,

KNOEDLER GALLERIES

Alfred Jacob Miller saw many mountain men and painted them superbly, as evidenced by these pictures. The view at right shows a trapper in full regalia; he had undoubtedly made his outfit himself. In the painting above, a trapper cleans his rifle as his dinner of buffalo ribs roasts and his mule stands by patiently.

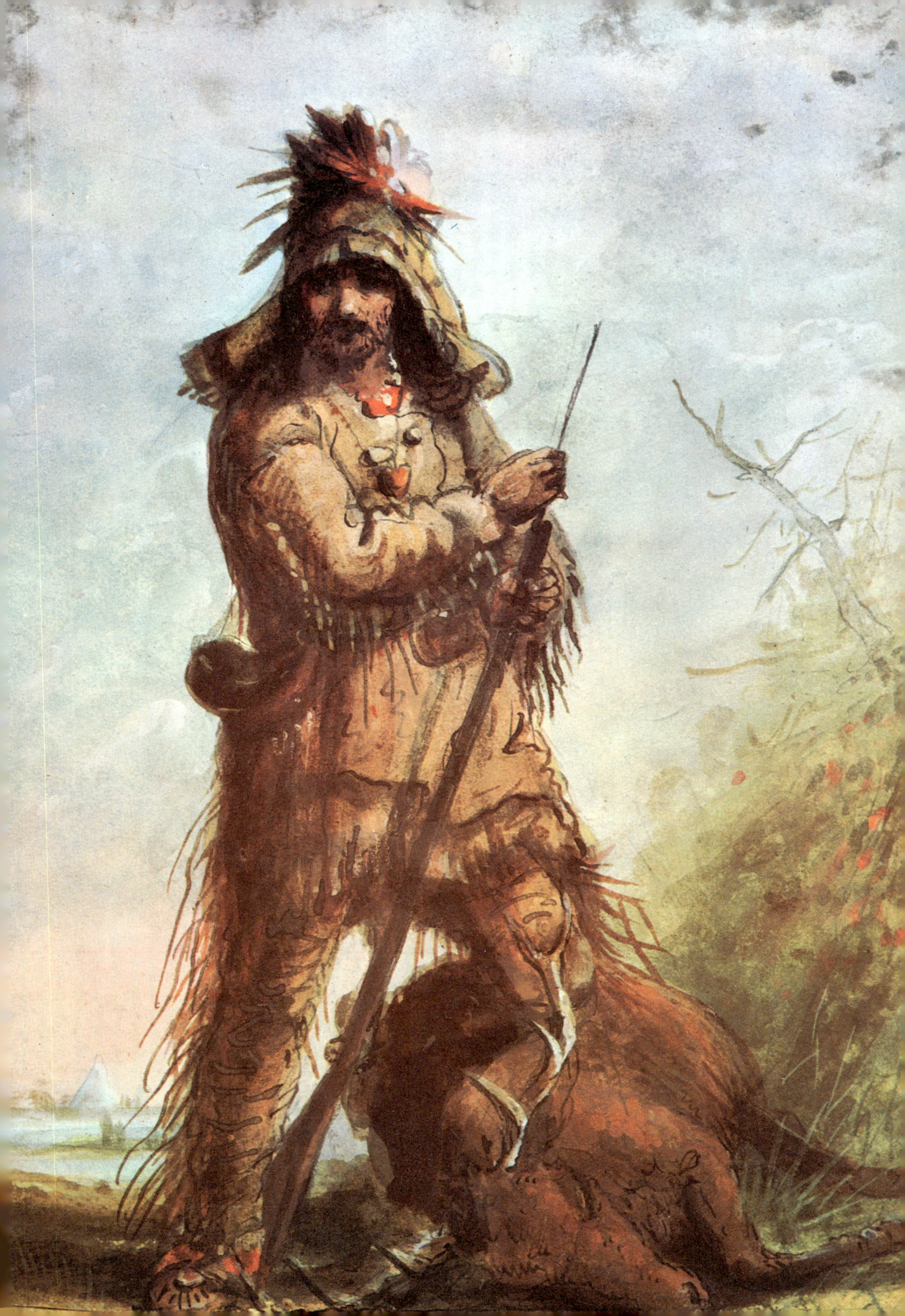

wintered in the mountains, and were reunited with their friends when Ashley brought out a supply train to the Green River in June, 1825. Ashley needed a mountain partner to direct the actual trapping operations and wisely offered Smith the post. Thus, within three years the raw recruit had advanced to a partnership. He returned with Ashley to St. Louis to outfit a winter supply train and recruit more trappers, and on October 30, with seventy men, 160 horses and mules, and $20,000 worth of trade goods, he headed west again.

At the first campsite, Smith divided his men into messes of eight or ten each. The leader of each mess was responsible for its supplies, well-being, and discipline. Each man had his saddle horse and pack mules, the remaining supplies being carried on mules. On reaching Indian country, Smith demanded great vigilance and order. After each mess was assigned its position in a campsite, a breastwork of packs and saddles was put up immediately. At sunset the horse guard picketed the animals close by. Fires were doused by nightfall, and sentries took up their positions. The mules made excellent sentinels, too, since they disliked the smell of Indians and acted up when any lurked about.

At daylight Smith and others scouted the area for Indians. Finding none, they aroused the camp and breakfasted. When it was time to travel, scouts ranged several miles in advance, on each side, and to the rear, ever on the alert. Such vigilance paid off. The larger parties almost never were attacked until they had crossed South Pass and split into small groups of four to eight for trapping.

When wagons did roll to Oregon, these traveling and camping methods worked out by Smith were generally followed. And Smith did more for future travelers. He is said to have blazed an important cutoff. Instead of following the left bank of the Missouri all the way up to the mouth of the Platte, he left the Missouri at its north bend and pushed westward briefly over the Santa Fe Trail to the mouth of the Kansas River. He forded the Kansas to reach the Little Blue, paralleled that stream past its headwaters, and went on to the Platte, about one hundred miles above its mouth. From there he went up the Platte to the Sweetwater, over South Pass, and down into the Green River drainage.

Beyond this was the interior basin trapped more than a decade earlier by Andrew Henry's parties, before Henry and Ashley became partners. Still westward stretched the complex Snake River drainage, honeycombed with trails and caches of the competing Britishers of the Hudson's Bay Company. Because the brawling, twisting Snake was a tributary of the Columbia, its drainage was considered part of the Oregon country.

Astoria, which President Jefferson had considered "the germ of a great, free, independent empire," had fallen to the British during the War of 1812.

KNOEDLER GALLERIES

Jim Bridger, the daring and adventurous mountain man, comes to life in this curious study by Miller. This is the earliest picture of Bridger; whether he was actually wearing armor, or whether Miller was merely being playful by showing him dressed that way, is unknown.

SCOTTS BLUFF NATIONAL MONUMENT

William H. Jackson's sketch shows the excitement and bustle of the departure of the Smith, Jackson, and Sublette trading caravan in May, 1830. The two dearborn carriages, followed by ten supply wagons, were the first vehicles to travel the Oregon Trail to the Rockies.

In 1818 it was restored to its owner. Astor offered to reoccupy the post if given a military force to defend it, but Congress failed to act, and so did the fur baron. That same year joint occupancy of the Oregon country by the United States and Great Britain was agreed upon.

Though other American companies were invading the beaver haunts west and north of South Pass, none were so expertly managed or so successful as the brigades directed by Jedediah Smith. In 1826 Ashley had made enough money to retire from the fur trade. He sold out to Smith and two cronies, William Sublette and David E. Jackson. The new firm made history in 1830 by being the first to haul wagons over the Oregon Trail to the mountains.

Since Smith preferred to remain in the mountains, it was Sublette who led out from St. Louis the eighty-man expedition mounted on mules. Included were ten wagons, which, unlike horses or mules, did not have to be unloaded every night. They were much smaller than the later canvas-topped prairie schooners of the great emigration period. Each carried about 1,800 pounds of supplies and was pulled by five mules. There were also two dearborns, light four-wheeled carriages, each drawn by a single mule.

The vehicles swayed, jolted, and mired down. Stream banks had to be cut back so they could reach water level to cross. Yet all got through safely, without serious delay, in thirteen weeks. Twelve steers and one milk cow also made the trip, the first cattle to arrive in the Rocky Mountains.

When Smith returned eastward with the wagons, starting August 4, 1830, he could not help noting the developments that had occurred since his first trip to the mountains eight years before. Settlers had pushed farther up and out from the Missouri's banks. Crude, weak Fort Atkinson had been replaced by bustling Fort Leavenworth. Steamboat traffic on the river had expanded greatly, giving rise to several new river towns, notably Independence, Missouri. As soon as men learned they could lop off 250 miles of slow, boggy road travel between St. Louis and Independence, that town (and later nearby Westport) became the favored jumping-off place for those heading out on the Oregon Trail.

Proud of having taken wagons west, Smith, Jackson, and Sublette wrote at length about their feat to the Secretary of War, John H. Eaton. True, their wagons went to the mountains only, not over them, because the firm's rendezvous, or trading fair, was held on the east slope of the Wind River range, near South Pass. But Smith stressed that the wagons could have continued "easily" all the way to Oregon.

Jedediah Smith was an excellent trapper and a brilliant explorer, but only a fair prophet. He was right that wagons would someday go all the way to Oregon—within a dozen years they would do just that. But they would never make the trip "easily."

The fur trade provided the push that first sent wagons west. It proved more practical to dispatch supplies to the Rockies by wagon than by pack animal. In Miller's painting of a trading caravan crossing the prairie, the ghostly mirage of a lake shimmers on the horizon.

WALTERS ART GALLERY; © 1951 UNIVERSITY OF OKLAHOMA PRESS

4.
Wagons over the Mountains

In 1832, two years after the Smith, Jackson, and Sublette wagons went to the mountains, St. Louis buzzed with new rumors. Captain Benjamin Louis Eulalie de Bonneville announced that he had been granted army leave to enter the cutthroat competition of the fur trade. He planned to take wagons across the mountains, perhaps even to the Columbia.

The French-born captain was a graduate of West Point, thirty-six years old, and a veteran of frontier army service in Arkansas and Oklahoma. He was also a seasoned prairie traveler. Nevertheless, his idea of taking wagons across the mountains was considered radical, if not downright foolish. For his assistants-in-command, he chose two tough and experienced mountain men, Michael Cerré and Joseph Reddeford Walker.

May is a fair month in Missouri, with enough young grass sprouted to feed horses and mules. Bonneville chose to start out May 1, 1832, from Fort Osage, a frontier post east of present-day Kansas City, Missouri. Accompanying him were 110 men and twenty wagons in a double column. Some of the wagons were drawn by four mules or horses, others by oxen, which were an innovation on the Oregon Trail, although long used on the Santa Fe Trail. The mounted men startled many small hamlets by riding through them pell-mell, with loud whooping and shooting.

Late every afternoon the wagons were drawn into a square, the thirty-foot gaps between them closed with chains or ropes. The animals were driven inside and well guarded during the night. As an extra precaution against bolting, or being stolen by Indians, each horse was "side-lined"— that is, the front and back legs on the same side were loosely tied together so as to allow slow moving about, but no running. The hunting along the wooded riverbanks was good, and those craving sweets made regular forays to locate wild honey.

In six days the Bonneville expedition had passed the last border habitation. Cold rains and mud now dampened the men's frolicking. Six more such days brought them to the Kansas River, men and animals jaded from overexertion. The last two weeks in May they lined out across the rolling Kansas plain, treeless, cut with rambling water courses, short on wild game and long on ninety-degree midday temperatures. It was naked and monotonous country, presenting few real difficulties for the wagons.

On June 2 the men sent up the shout, "Ho, the coasts of Nebraska!" heralding their first view of the Platte River. Although from one to three miles wide and three to six feet deep, the muddy, sluggish stream was bottomed with quicksand that made fording impossible. Only on Grand Island and other midstream islands were there any cottonwood trees or willows.

Bonneville moved on up the south bank. The valley grade lifted steadily. Not far above the Platte's forks, he ordered the wheels removed from the wagons and the sides waterproofed with buffalo hides and a compound of tallow and ashes. With three men riding each wagon-boat to pole it, others pushed the clumsy barks across the South Platte. To cross an intervening nine miles of sand, the wheels had to be put on again and the oxen pinned to their yokes; then all had to be undone again to get across the swift, six-hundred-yard-wide North Platte. Riders led the mules across because their small hooves made them easy prey to quicksand. The men learned, too, that once a mule got water in its

DENVER PUBLIC LIBRARY WESTERN COLLECTION

Following his adventures in the Rockies, Captain Bonneville won a promotion for bravery during the Mexican War. He is shown here near the end of his Army career.

WALTERS ART GALLERY; © 1951 UNIVERSITY OF OKLAHOMA PRESS

These Indian warriors, sketched by Miller as they swooped down on a wagon train, wanted goods rather than scalps. The Indians felt that the white men ought to pay them in some way for the privilege of crossing their tribal lands. It was always dangerous to refuse their demands.

ears it often panicked and died in its tracks. No matter how slow, progress, not speed, was the order of the day.

Up the North Platte they went, where a beautiful grove of cottonwoods and the sight of buffalo lightened the men's spirits. The hunt was wild and exhilarating. It was good to have a wood fire again. But soon they began to get a hint of what lay ahead. The ascending plains rolled and heaved; high bluffs thrust up abruptly. They passed a rock column shooting straight up from the plain for 150 feet. This was Chimney Rock, famed landmark of a later day, some 550 miles out from their starting point.

Wheel tracks clearly marked their passage among other "beetling" cliffs and around the base of Scotts Bluff, named for an ailing trapper deserted there to die by his comrades. From its craggy haunts they brought down a mountain bighorn sheep, white-wooled, with a beard like a nanny goat.

On June 24 scouts galloped back shouting, "To arms! Indians!" Captain Bonneville ordered the wagons into a square and the men to battle stations— none too soon. Sixty Crow warriors rode down on them, charging toward the train but swerving at the last moment to right and left and then wheeling in a wide circle. Having displayed their prowess, finery, and superb horsemanship, the Indians dismounted. The chief extended the peace pipe, and he and Bonneville smoked. The Crows revealed that they had had the train under surveillance for days.

They were astonished to see wagons and the lone cow and calf tagging at the rear. Were they tame buffalo? Might they examine them?

Bonneville assented. The Crows petted the calf, examined the wheels, and made friendly overtures to the whites. They embraced them and rubbed greasy cheeks against bearded ones— and slyly emptied the travelers' pockets, even cutting the metal buttons from their jackets. Thievery was high art and great sport among the Crows, and many other items lying about disappeared before they departed, smiling and vowing eternal friendship.

The dry air was easy to breathe and fragrant with sage, but it shrank the woodwork on the wagon boxes and the spokes on the wheels. In toiling through the broken country of eastern Wyoming, the train teetered in and out of one ravine after another, while the stony road wore out the horses' shoes. Bonneville's men had not yet learned the Crow trick of covering the hooves with buffalo hide.

On July 12 the leader turned away from the North Platte and moved through loose sand for two days before reaching the Sweetwater. Here fragmented hills were coming together to form lengthy, lofty ranges; isolated blocks of rock thrusting high from the plains forced the travelers to make wide circuits around them. This was the gateway to the Rocky Mountains, long anticipated but not yet seen. Not until they topped a ridge on July 20 did they see the towering Wind River

Mountain man Joe Walker, Bonneville's chief scout and explorer during the Captain's three-year stay in the mountains, is shown with his Indian wife in this Miller painting.

Mountains with their snowy crests. North, west, and south— all was mountain country, exciting and a little frightening.

The animals were sore-footed, the men weary of so many weeks in the saddle, and the wagons almost fallen apart. But the men cheered when Bonneville indicated their goal lay a short distance away, on the far side of the Wind River peaks. However, something had to be done about the wheels or the train would grind to a permanent halt. A drastic remedy was tried: the iron tires were taken off, bands of wood nailed around the outside of the felloes, the tires heated and replaced, and the whole dropped into cold water. The hot iron contracted rapidly against the moisture-swollen wood, and the wheels were sturdy again.

They toiled ever upward, and now, though it was just past mid-July, there was ice in the water buckets every morning. It took seven and a half hours to cross the easy slope of South Pass. That night the men caught trout in a little stream whose waters flowed toward the Pacific Ocean. For the first time, wagons had crossed the Continental Divide.

On July 27, 1832, Bonneville halted in a grassy meadow alongside the Green River. It was the end of the line for the wagons. Here the ex-West Pointer built a crude log fort, dispatched his trappers, and prepared to trade with the Indians. But life as an army officer had not prepared him to survive the ungentlemanly competition of rival traders, particularly Astor's American Fur Company, camped nearby. They out-trapped and out-traded him and hired his men away. Worse, they dubbed his fort Bonneville's Folly and Fort Nonsense.

Nonsense it was not, we know now, following research into his papers. Fort Bonneville was plumb center of the beaver country. Men traveling east or west, north or south, passed close enough for the Captain to note who they were and what their business was. Of the six hundred trappers estimated in the West, too many were British, he thought. Though his wagons stopped short of Oregon, his observance of British activities did not. His parties ranged deeply into the Oregon country and even into California. For three more years Bonneville labored diligently as trader and secret intelligence officer, reporting regularly to officials in Washington. When he emerged from the mountains in August, 1835, the competition had bankrupted him. But he found fame, if not fortune, after *The Adventures of Captain Bonneville*, Washington Irving's book based on his experiences, was published in 1837.

Irving's book helped bring Oregon and the Oregon Trail into the public mind. Congressmen, editors, and others debated the "Oregon question," demanding that the United States cancel its joint occupancy with Great Britain. A showdown would have to wait, however, until many more wagons had deepened the ruts from Independence to Fort Walla Walla.

KNOEDLER GALLERIES

The teams in Alfred Jacob Miller's sketch are pulling two-wheeled charettes up a steep riverbank. The charette was one of the smallest and lightest wagons used in the West.

This eerie spot is a Chinook burial ground. For centuries these Indians of the Oregon country had placed their dead in raised canoes and on platforms as a matter of religious belief. The missionaries who came west attempted to replace such ancient rites with Christian practices.

DETROIT INSTITUTE OF ARTS

5.
Missionaries to the Heathen

In 1833 a curious letter published in *The Christian Advocate and Journal* brought forth a new sort of pioneer to the Oregon Trail. The letter related how one Flathead and three Nez Perce Indians had journeyed to St. Louis in search of the "white man's Book of Heaven." They had placed their request before William Clark, co-captain of the Lewis and Clark expedition and now Superintendent of Indian Affairs. Clark promised that someday a teacher would come to them.

Illustrating the letter was a sketch of an Indian whose forehead slanted back in a straight line to the crown, the result of unnatural bandaging in infancy. Supposedly this barbaric deformation was practiced by the Flathead tribe that lived west of the Continental Divide. In spite of the sketch being absolutely false (the Chinooks were the ones who did this), it raised a great hue and cry among zealous Methodist and Presbyterian missionaries, who hastened to be the first to bring Christianity to the heathen.

The Nez Perces and Flatheads were superior Indians, friendly to the whites since first visited by Lewis and Clark and the Astorians. From them and from later traders they heard about God, the Sabbath, and the Bible. They gained the idea that the white man's power was centered in his religion; therefore, they concluded, to gain more power for themselves, they must learn about Christianity. By power, they meant goods: beads, awls, blankets, muskets, and metal articles. They were not interested in Christian salvation, only in the strong "medicine" that would bring them more of the white man's goods and guns and, thus, victory over their enemies. The missionaries, intent on saving souls, never did understand this Indian concept of Christianity.

The idea of Christianizing the Indians of Oregon had been introduced as early as 1824 by a Boston schoolmaster named Hall Jackson Kelley. Kelley also thumped for colonizing the Oregon region so as to strengthen American claims to it. He published pamphlets and lectured tirelessly; he even tried to form a company of his own to travel to Oregon. When this plan fell apart, he started for Oregon on his own by the sea route.

Meanwhile, the letter in *The Christian Advocate* was bearing fruit. To meet the great challenge and carry the Word of God west, the Methodists selected a tall, hearty, thirty-one-year-old evangelist named Jason Lee. As a co-worker, Lee chose his nephew Daniel Lee. Both had zeal and energy, but they knew nothing about Oregon.

Fortunately, they now met Nathaniel J. Wyeth, a prosperous New England merchant, just returned from a trip to the Oregon country. Although failing to make any money in the fur trade, Wyeth had brought back two half-breed Indian lads whose heads were not really flat, but flatter than most. Pointing to the "deformed" Indian boys, Wyeth and the two Lees made public appeals for money; pitying New Englanders opened their purses, and funds for a missionary expedition rolled in.

In the spring of 1834, Wyeth, Jason and Daniel Lee, and a pair of scientists, Thomas Nuttall and John Kirk Townsend, who wanted to study the flora and fauna of the West, set out on the Oregon Trail. At the Green River they met Thomas Fitzpatrick, the famed pathfinder and survivor of hair-raising encounters with Indians and grizzlies, and rode with him to Ham's Fork and a spectacular rendezvous. There they mingled with the elite of the fur trade, including Jim Bridger and Kit Carson, and a Scottish nobleman-adventurer, Captain William Drummond Stewart. The West was no longer the private domain of the mountain men and the Indians. Thanks to the Oregon Trail, shadows of civilization—missionaries, scientists, sportsmen—were already lengthening across the continent.

A delegation of Nez Perces and Flatheads arrived, dressed in their finest. The Indians had journeyed far in the hope of meeting the teacher of the religion that would make them rich and powerful. Jason Lee palavered briefly with the Indians he was charged with Christianizing.

Lee then announced an astonishing decision. He chose not to travel north with the Flatheads. Though his diary gives little clue to his behavior, he wrote later, "The truth is they are *Indians*." Possibly he meant that these Indians, however amenable, were still

An 1833 sketch of an Indian with a flattened forehead stirred the missionaries to action.

savages in a violent land, dealing with whites who were themselves half-wild and godless. Perhaps he felt that they could be converted only after long association with whites who farmed, raised families, and lived a Christian way of life.

After the rendezvous, Wyeth, the Lees, the two scientists, and Captain Stewart moved out into a barren land, hilly, desolate, and pocked with outcroppings of black lava. On the Snake River, Wyeth built a fur post. Naming it Fort Hall after one of his backers, he ran up a frail American flag made of "bleached sheeting, a little red flannel, and a few blue patches." At the mouth of the Boise River was a rival Hudson's Bay Company post, Fort Boise. But none could know, this far out on the frontier, that the death knell of the mountain beaver trade had already sounded. Fickle fashion no longer favored the beaver hat; the demand that brought high prices and

GILCREASE INSTITUTE

Many of the missionaries, including the Lees and the Whitmans, paused on their way to Oregon to marvel at colorful and exciting fur traders' rendezvous such as this one.

fabulous fortunes was petering out. Like Fort Hall, Fort Boise would soon save many a desperate family on its way to Oregon.

The company finally reached another Hudson's Bay post, Fort Walla Walla, on September 2, 1834. A two-week journey down the Columbia took them to Fort Vancouver, where they found the emaciated, feverish Hall Jackson Kelley. Embittered by misfortune and illness, Kelley would soon return east, his dream shattered. He was a prophet born too soon.

For Nathaniel Wyeth, as for Captain Bonneville, the Oregon Trail was the road to business failure. For the scientists Nuttall and Townsend, it was a long, happy highway through a naturalist's paradise. For Jason Lee, the Trail's end forced a momentous decision. He paddled up the Willamette River for sixty miles, where he saw farms, flocks, sawmills, and orchards established largely by Americans who had arrived by the sea route. He saw, too, Indians already adopting white men's ways — and Chinooks with flattened heads.

From the mission he built on the Willamette he wrote many letters urging the Methodist Mission Board to send him families, farmers, workmen, machinery, seeds, and fruit saplings. From this moment on, Jason Lee divided his energies between missionary work and colonization. Ultimately he would be dismissed from his church post for having sacrificed religion to more material matters.

A middle-aged Congregational minister, the Reverend Samuel Parker, had also been deeply moved to read in *The Christian Advocate* of the Indians' plea for missionaries. Too late to head west with the Lees, he spent a year collecting funds and workers to leave in May of 1835. One of his recruits was a none-too-sturdy, thirty-three-year-old Presbyterian doctor named Marcus Whitman. Though untidy and rough in speech and manners, Dr. Whitman offset this with kindness, patience, and a sincere desire to serve the Indians.

Parker and Whitman departed from Liberty, Missouri, with the annual supply train of the American Fur Company, headed by Lucien Fontenelle. Fontenelle and his men were hostile to the missionaries at first, considering them "meddlesome do-gooders." But after Whitman helped with the arduous trail work, putting his shoulder to mired-down wagons, helping build crude bridges and rafts, and even lightening a wagon load when necessary by carrying his bedding and tent, he won their grudging respect.

One night, after nearly a month on the Trail, Dr. Whitman was routed out of his blankets to tend a sick man. He immediately recognized the ailment as cholera, the dread scourge that had killed hundreds of thousands abroad and was now reaching out to the American frontier. It struck swiftly and violently and killed within hours.

The presence of cholera almost panicked the men. Some were sure to die, and the caravan might be so devastated

This painted warrior and three companions went to St. Louis in 1831 to learn about Christianity.

that it would never reach the mountains. By morning others were toppling over with severe cramps and retching. Dr. Whitman set to work. For twelve days and nights he battled the disease, keeping those who were stricken warm and full of fluids. He had the camp moved to clean ground and demanded more sanitary measures. Three men died, and Fontenelle himself nearly went under, when suddenly the attacks stopped, and there was no more cholera. When they were rolling again, Fontenelle extended "the kindest treatment" to the doctor.

Perhaps because of his age, or because he controlled the purse strings, Parker did little. It was the exhausted Whitman who packed and unpacked their animals, raised the tent, and did the cooking.

Beyond Fort Laramie the caravan was led by Thomas Fitzpatrick. Lean, weathered, a Hawken rifle readied across his saddle, his eyes inflamed from the alkali dust and the never-ending lookout for Indians, the taciturn mountain man took them over South Pass. At the trappers' rendezvous on the Green, the missionaries met Jim Bridger and saw Kit Carson's gun fight with Bully Shunar.

Bully was aptly named. Pugnacious and bigmouthed, he challenged anyone present to fight him. Carson accepted, mounted, cocked his pistol, and rushed to meet Shunar. Both fired almost simultaneously. Shunar missed, but Carson's bullet entered Bully's hand, came out at the wrist, and then passed through his upper arm. He begged for his life, and Carson obliged.

With trappers and Indians looking on, Dr. Whitman removed a three-inch barbed iron arrowhead which Bridger had had imbedded in his back for three years. After this, others stepped forward for medical treatment of various sorts. Whitman also met Captain Stewart. The dapper Scottish nobleman took delivery on a light cart of luxuries he had ordered from St. Louis: expensive woolens, Manton guns, preserved fruits, cheeses, potted meats, and fine liquors. The appurtenances of soft living were making their appearance on the Trail.

Whitman and Parker palavered with a Nez Perce and Flathead delegation, different from the one Jason Lee had rejected but still hopeful of meeting the teacher they had been promised. Fitzpatrick described fully the home grounds of both tribes, where a mission could best be located, and the rich resources of timber, water, and pasture land in the Nez Perce country. These resources were vital, for any fledgling mission needed to be self-supporting.

Since the Mission Board had charged them only with finding whether a mission among the Indians was possible and desirable, and where it should be built, the missionaries decided Parker should go on to the Nez Perce country to survey sites; Whitman would return east to recruit workers and materials.

Back east the good doctor enrolled the Reverend and Mrs. Henry Harmon Spalding in the cause. However dedicated and religious, Spalding proved to be an ill-tempered, peevish sort who was critical of nearly everything. Even the patient Whitman found himself sorely tried by this man.

On February 18, 1836, Whitman married golden-haired Narcissa Prentiss. Twenty-seven, well-educated for a woman of the time, propelled into the missionary calling by a religious revival then sweeping New England, Narcissa viewed Indians in far too romantic a light. Yet she must have recognized the real danger ahead because she wore black at her wedding, and in her fine voice, resolutely sang:

> Yes, my native land, I love thee,
> All thy scenes I love them well.
> Friends, connections, happy country,
> Now, I bid you all farewell.

At Cincinnati the Whitmans met their trail companions, the stern Spalding and his mousy, sad-eyed wife, Eliza.

The Yellowstone, *painted here by George Catlin as it chugged past St. Louis in 1832, was the first steamboat to carry missionaries and fur traders up the Missouri River.*

George Catlin, whose paintings would provide future generations with a colorful record of the prairie and Indians, had warned Spalding that the journey to the mountains was full of great hardships and unspeakable horrors for white women. But Catlin could have saved his breath, for Narcissa and Eliza were not turning back.

The two couples embarked on a steamboat for the journey to St. Louis, and from there, up the Missouri to Liberty. The women fashioned a large, tepee-shaped tent of striped, oiled bedticking. Whitman purchased a heavy farm wagon to hold supplies needed for the Trail and for setting up their mission, and to carry Narcissa's small

65

JESUS CHRIST.

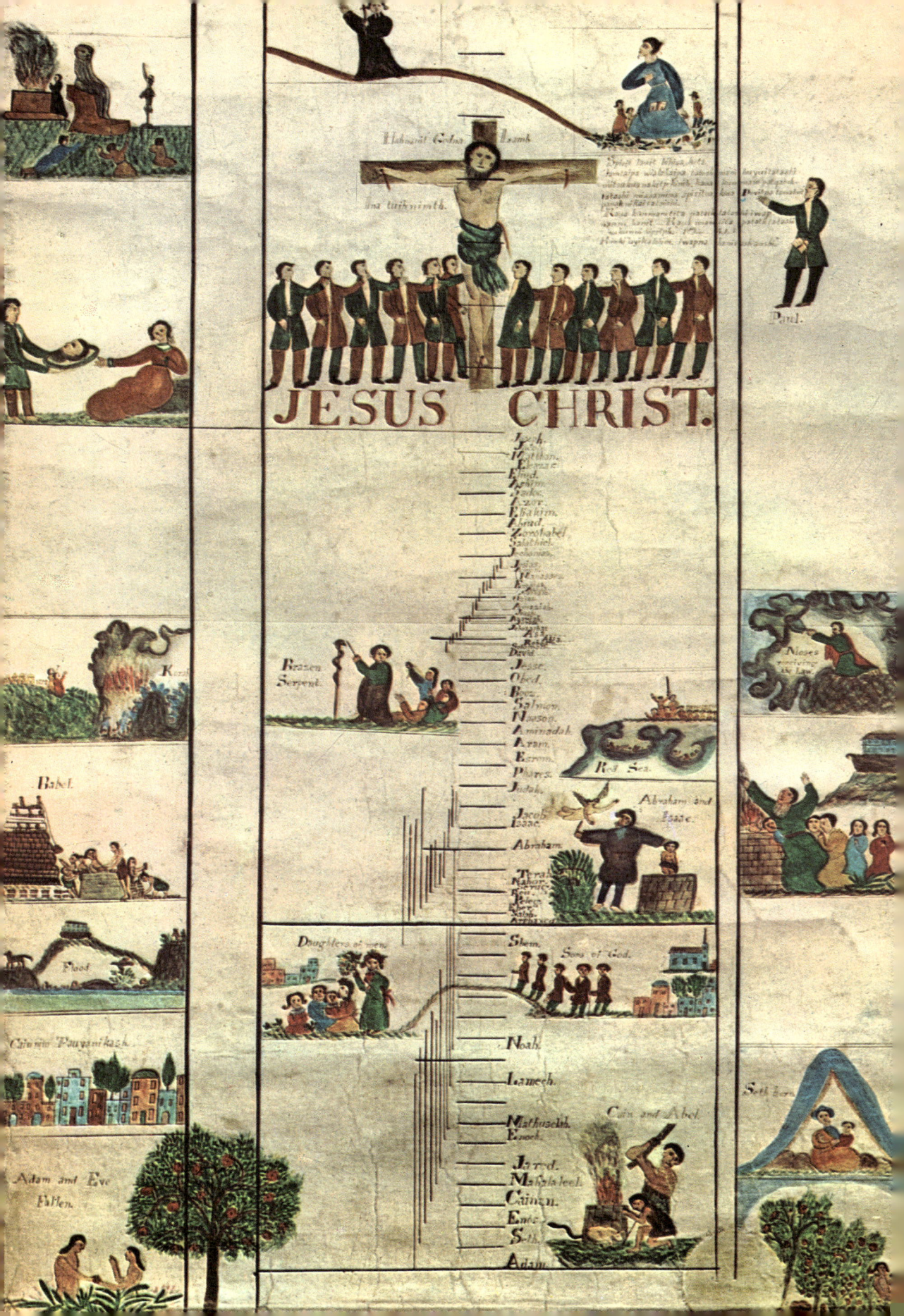

Joseph
Matthan
Eleazar
Eliud
Achim
Sadoc
Azor
Eliakim
Abiud
Zorobabel
Salathiel
Jechonias
Josias
Amon
Manasses
Ezekias
Achaz
Joatham
Ozias
Joram
Josaphat
Asa
Abia
Roboam
David
Jesse
Obed
Booz
Salmon
Naason
Aminadab
Aram
Esrom
Phares
Judah
Jacob
Isaac
Abraham
Terah
Nahor
Serug
Reu
Peleg
Heber
Salah
Arphaxad
Shem
Noah
Lamech
Mathuselah
Enoch
Jared
Mahalaleel
Cainan
Enos
Seth
Adam

Paul.

Moses receiving the Law.

Red Sea.

Abraham and Isaac.

Brazen Serpent.

Daughters of men. Sons of God.

Cain and Abel.

Seth born.

Babel.

Flood.

Adam and Eve Fallen.

trunk of bright calico dresses and her portable writing box. He also bought twelve horses, six mules, and seventeen head of cattle. The Spaldings had a light wagon with yellow wheels in which to carry their baggage and Eliza's box of water paints and paper.

Forty miles above Fort Leavenworth the Whitman party gained a volunteer handyman. Carefree, threadbare sixteen-year-old Miles Goodyear appeared "from Iowa." He aimed to be a mountain man. Somewhere up ahead was the American Fur Company's caravan led by Thomas Fitzpatrick. The pace was not leisurely; at times, in fact, it was intolerable, but the Whitman party finally caught up.

Narcissa thrived on wilderness travel. She wore men's heavy boots and a full skirt, rode sidesaddle, and penned her enthusiasms in detail in a journal. Meanwhile, Spalding became increasingly difficult, and Eliza grew more sallow, more frail, more resigned to a trailside grave.

Missionaries in the Far West, both Protestant and Catholic, tried many ways of explaining the history and meaning of Christianity to the Indians. This pictorial chart is part of the "Protestant Ladder," a teaching device for the Indians designed by Henry Spalding and drawn by his wife Eliza. The complete chart is six feet long. The central panel pictures the development of Christianity, culminating with Christ on the Cross. The twelve disciples wear neat, nineteenth-century business suits. The right-hand column shows the upward path to Heaven, topped by the figure of St. Paul. Sinners who strayed from the path of righteousness ended up in the left-hand column, the road to Hell.

"Turn out, turn out!" The familiar call roused the camp at dawn. Soon the caravan moved out—seventy men, four hundred animals, and seven big wagons each drawn by six mules. From leader Fitzpatrick to the last bawling calf, the line stretched for a mile.

Narcissa's entry for June 3, 1836, reads: "Start usually at six, travel till eleven, encamp, rest and feed, start again about two, travel until six or before, then encamp for the night." At Fort Laramie the ladies thrilled to the sight of buildings and rested on chairs cushioned with buffalo hide. They did a sizable laundry. "Husband," as Narcissa referred to the doctor in her diary, had hoped to take the wagons all the way to the Columbia. But she had to write entries like "Husband has had a tedious time with the wagon today" all too often. Regretfully, Marcus abandoned the lumbering farm wagon, transferring its freight to mules.

When Captain Stewart and two other gentlemen joined the caravan, Narcissa invited them to tea. Alongside the Trail she spread India-rubber sheeting for a ground cloth and did her best to keep sand from blowing in the "tin basens." Though long-used to raw whiskey, the gentlemen observed the amenities. And tea it was, brewed in a syrup can with water from a mountain stream. Nighttimes, the men delighted Narcissa with preposterous tales told around the roaring campfire, while the vivacious bride sat on the ground, or on Husband's knees.

ARCHIVES, MISSOURI PROVINCE, SOCIETY OF JESUS

Before starting on a hunt, these Flathead Indians, painted by the Catholic missionary Father Nicholas Point, hold up their weapons to be blessed by the priest at top center.

This 1849 water color shows the Methodist mission and stockade at The Dalles, on the Columbia River. Jason Lee and his followers first established a mission here in 1837.

Fitzpatrick, heading full speed for the trappers' rendezvous on the Green, delayed long enough for Narcissa and Eliza to scratch their names on Independence Rock. This was a huge granite formation that had gotten its name when Fitzpatrick cached some furs there on or about July 4, 1824. It was a favorite landmark on the Trail, where passers-by stopped to inscribe their names in the stone. In time it gained the reputation of being the great "register" of the Oregon Trail.

On this Fourth of July, 1836, the missionaries topped South Pass. Recalling the event years later, Spalding claimed that "they, alighting from their horses and kneeling on the other half of the continent, with the Bible in one hand and the American flag in the other, took possession of it as the home of American mothers, and of the Church of Christ." Actually, there was no kneeling, no flag, nothing more than the usual dusty crossing.

At the Green River rendezvous the missionaries saw some fifteen Indian tribes in their gaudiest, strutting best and four hundred uninhibited mountain men. Squaws swarmed around the two women, fingering their dresses and white skins and Narcissa's golden hair. But it was Eliza they warmed to. Face to face with real, not very noble Indians, Narcissa's romantic notions died hard. She withdrew, preferring to watch the races, sham battles, and dancing of the mountain men.

When a Hudson's Bay Company caravan came in, it brought Whitman his first word from Parker. The two were to have met at the rendezvous, but Parker was off viewing the upper Columbia and suggested only that Whitman continue west with the Britishers. He did so. Beyond lay a wild country, yet none of his party, not even the women, seemed fearful as they rode out on the worst part of the journey.

The scrawny cattle had to be goaded constantly. The light, yellow-wheeled wagon was still with them, but only because Whitman refused to abandon it. This first wheeled vehicle to travel the Oregon Trail beyond the rendezvous site mired down, upset, slowed progress, tried tempers, and finally splintered an axletree. Whitman converted it to a two-wheeled cart and labored on to Fort Hall. The ladies were disappointed. There were no cushioned chairs inside the cramped log walls and no windows, and the vegetable garden had gone to seed.

Beyond Fort Hall they lost the trail and plodded across swampland where clouds of mosquitoes swarmed over them. The soaring peaks faded in the distance as they followed the Snake. The sagebrush grew three feet high and made progress difficult. They were exhausted when, two weeks later, they reached Fort Boise. Learning that still worse traveling lay ahead, Whitman finally abandoned the cart. So Jed Smith's contention of 1830, that wagons could "easily" travel to the Columbia, had run afoul of the awful reality of rocks, rivers, and deserts. Even Narcissa's bright spirit flagged during the next three terrible weeks, and Eliza resigned herself to death. Yet somehow they finally reached Fort Walla Walla.

How wonderful to sit in a cushioned chair, to eat pork, potatoes, melons, butter, bread! When a rooster crowed, Narcissa almost wept for joy. A swift boat trip brought them to Fort Vancouver. Here Marcus learned to his bitter disappointment that Parker had sailed for home.

However, Parker's *Journal of an Exploring Tour Beyond the Rocky Mountains* proved to be one of the best guidebooks for later emigrants and convinced some at least that families could travel the Oregon Trail with comparative safety. In it Parker also dared suggest that the Indians should be safeguarded from the white man's diseases and alcohol and granted protection for their basic rights and their land. They were noble thoughts, and completely ignored.

Once assured that the missionaries planned to preach and not to colonize, John McLoughlin, the benevolent head of the Hudson's Bay Company operations in Oregon, furnished supplies and a boat for the men to return upriver to select their mission sites. By now the Whitmans and the Spaldings could scarcely tolerate each other's company. Spalding settled among the Nez Perces at Lapwai, or Butterfly Valley, in what is now Idaho, while Whitman chose a location at Waiilatpu, "the Place of the Rye Grass," among the Cayuse tribe.

The Whitmans would spend eleven difficult, frustrating years of grueling labor building a mission and a school and bringing Christianity and civilized living to Waiilatpu. They caused other missionaries to enter the Oregon mission field. More important, since Narcissa and Eliza had, against all odds, survived the overland trek, other white women dared try.

A conviction that it was their "manifest destiny . . . to overspread the continent" drew many to the Oregon Trail. That conviction was tested severely by the harsh and lonely western landscape shown in this painting of a wagon train fording a creek near Fort Laramie.

COLLECTION OF HALL PARK MCCULLOUGH

6.
A Highway of Destiny

The "Oregon question" was mushrooming into a national debate by 1838. The Oregon Trail was beginning to be viewed as a highway of destiny, a highway to carry a flood tide of Americans to nail down a continent.

This state of mind fitted neatly into Jason Lee's plans. He had grandiose ideas about peopling Oregon with Methodists. He was eager to raise money and recruits by lecturing his way from the Midwest to New York City, the headquarters of the Methodist Mission Board. When the Willamette Valley settlers, anxiously awaiting civil law and justice that would protect them and their property, drafted a petition demanding these rights from Congress, they entrusted Jason Lee with the important task of delivering the petition to Washington.

On March 28, 1838, Lee placed the precious paper in a small metal box and packed it with other necessities in a traveling bag. He canoed down the Willamette to the Columbia and up the Columbia to The Dalles. There he inspected the station established by his nephew Daniel Lee and a co-worker. Having mastered enough Chinook jargon, he preached to the Indians assembled there.

On April 14 he appeared at the Whitman Mission. He showed the good doctor the petition and revealed his great plans for extending Methodist missions throughout the Oregon country. When Lee departed, he carried a letter that Whitman and Spalding wrote to their own Mission Board, requesting 220 helpers—missionaries, farm workers, schoolteachers, physicians, and merchants, plus books, tools, hardware, and a flour mill—all desperately needed if the Presbyterians and Congregationalists were to keep apace of the Methodist expansion.

By July, Lee had reached the fur trade rendezvous on the Popo Agie River. The great celebrations were a thing of the past. He met only a small group of trappers and an adventurer named Captain John Augustus Sutter. Sutter was bound for California and a firm place in history; gold would be discovered in 1848 in the tailrace of his sawmill alongside the American River, setting off the greatest gold stampede the world had ever seen.

Lee also met a missionary party, westbound for Waiilatpu, consisting of four newlywed couples and one bachelor. The march to Oregon was picking up. The leader was a disagreeable fellow named William Gray, who had started with the Whitmans and then turned back. Gray and his wife Mary, Asa and Sarah Smith, Elkanah and Mary Walker, Cushing and Myra Eells, and the bachelor Cornelius Rogers somehow kept their party intact despite constant and bitter bickering.

After Lee waved them off, the missionaries headed for Fort Hall without escort. Soon, Asa Smith collapsed on the blistering plain. The others moved on, leaving the defenseless Sarah to hold the horses and tend her supposedly dying husband. Fortunately, the veteran trapper Joe Meek came along.

After one look at Smith, he decided on a drastic remedy. "If you want to stay here and be scalped, you can stay. Mrs. Smith is going with me," Meek told the prostrate man. While Sarah protested, Meek grabbed her horse's reins and led her away. But as Meek guessed, before they were out of sight Smith was up and following, and before dark the entire company was reunited.

The Whitmans were astonished when the newcomers straggled into Waiilatpu. They had not been expected but were most welcome. What joy to have news from home, to learn who was President! As hostess, Narcissa made them as comfortable as possible. She offered fresh milk, melons and potatoes from the garden, and pumpkin pies. The men organized the Oregon Mission of the American Board and held lengthy meetings from which their wives were excluded.

The ladies did as ladies have for ages whenever a few gathered — they formed a women's club. On September 3, 1838, the Columbia Maternal Association was duly organized, with Eliza Spalding as president, Mary Walker as vice-president, Mary Gray as recording secretary, Narcissa Whitman as corresponding secretary, and Myra Eells and Sarah Smith as members. A constitution and bylaws were agreed upon. Since the members could not meet regularly, they agreed to commune through prayer on the second and fourth Wednesday of each month.

Meanwhile, back east, Jason Lee was exciting audiences with impassioned pleas that Americans rise up, take to the Trail, drive the British out of Oregon, and gain undisputed control of this wonderland of untold riches. The listeners applauded, gave money, and felt new stirrings of patriotism.

However, there was no headlong rush along the Trail. A severe economic depression, the so-called Panic of 1837,

Anna Pittman had her portrait painted for her parents before going to Oregon in 1836 to marry Jason Lee, whom she had never met. She died in childbirth just two years later.

75

had brought about many bank and small business failures, foreclosures of farm mortgages, and poor prices for farm crops. For the discouraged and near-destitute, Oregon beckoned as a Promised Land. But the Midwest was a long way from Oregon. A man could not just pull up stakes and hit the Trail alone; he had to have money for supplies and transportation. The poor began to scrimp and save for that day.

There were others, however, who could afford to indulge their craving for change and excitement. Mostly young men, they warmed to the respectable idea of enlisting in a patriotic crusade. Lee so thrilled such a group in Peoria, Illinois, that they formed their own migration company, the Oregon Dragoons. Their goal was to take possession of the disputed Oregon territory and break the hold of the Hudson's Bay Company.

The leader of the Dragoons, Thomas Jefferson Farnham, wrote later of their preparations: "Bacon and flour, salt

The Whitman mission, sketched by a visitor, included (from left) a mill, a guesthouse, a blacksmith shop, and the combination school and living quarters for Marcus and Narcissa.

and pepper, sufficient for four hundred miles, were secured in sacks; our powder-casks were wrapped in painted canvas, and large oil-cloths were purchased to protect these and our sacks of clothing from the rains." Guns were checked, bullets were molded, powder horns and cap boxes filled, and "all else done that was deemed needful, before we struck our tents for the Indian territory." Mrs. Farnham fashioned a company flag and painted on it the motto, "Oregon or the Grave."

The Dragoons blithely assumed that beyond four hundred miles they could live on game meat, though not one of the company was an experienced hunter. This gay, optimistic group of fifteen departed from Peoria in April, 1839. The ordinary discomfort of trail travel sharpened tempers, and several dropped out at Independence. Though the Trail as far as the Kansas River was well-traveled, the burning desire to win Oregon for America cooled as they moved deep into Indian country. Rain, mud, insects, and monotonous food further decimated the Dragoons. Farnham finally made it to Oregon, but did not tarry long. California lured him, but it also proved dismal. His discouraging letters, published in Midwestern newspapers, caused the collapse of more than one company enlisting members to travel to the rainbow's end.

The lure of free land in the Oregon country excited many would-be pioneers, such as Virginia-born Joel Walker. Brother of the famous mountain man Joseph Reddeford Walker, Joel was no stranger to frontiering. He had broken land in Tennessee and Missouri before Oregon beckoned. In the spring of 1840 Walker, his wife, and five children set out in two wagons in company with a small party of Presbyterian missionaries. They left their wagons at Fort Hall and continued on foot and horseback to Oregon. Joel Walker was the first to dare the rigors of the Oregon Trail in order to farm the Promised Land.

It was mid-1840 before Marcus Whitman saw wagon wheels roll into the mission yard at Waiilatpu. Months earlier, four destitute trappers had met at Fort Hall. The good old fur trade days were over, and to survive a man had to settle on land. Three of the cronies, Joe Meek, Doc Newell, and Caleb Wilkins, had married Nez Perce sisters. Along with Francis Ermatinger, they decided to settle in the Willamette Valley, transporting their few belongings in the wagons the Walker family had abandoned at Fort Hall.

Sagebrush, "higher than the mules' backs," and the steep terrain proved too much for even these tough veterans. Before long they discarded the wagon beds and lashed their goods to the running gear. It was still slow going, and both humans and animals were exhausted by the time they dragged into the mission yard. Whitman's hospitality recharged their energies. Newell was not impressed with their being the first to haul wagons that far west. He did not think it was worth the effort. But Whitman enthused: "You will never regret it. You have broken the ice, and when others see that wagons have passed, they too will pass, and in a few years the valley will be full of our people."

Whitman was right. Other wagons would roll into the Place of the Rye Grass as the march to Oregon swelled. On May 14, 1842, a large party left Elm Grove, southwest of Independence. Eighteen big white-topped wagons "winding down the long hill, followed by an immense train of horses, mules, cattle, drivers walking by their side, merrily singing or whistling"— thus a Miss Allen wrote in her diary of the departure of this train under the leadership of Elijah White.

The pompous, talkative White was no stranger to western Oregon, having arrived via the sea route to serve as physician at Jason Lee's Willamette mission. He and Lee quarreled, and White made ready to sail home. The settlers, disappointed because Congress had not acted on their petition, and feeling very much like orphans, urged Dr. White to carry their story to Congress. He did so, with long-winded oratory. The legislators agreed to dispatch an Indian agent to look after problems occurring between "the natives and citizens of the United States." They commissioned White for the position and ordered him to proceed overland immediately to his new post.

White headed west, lecturing as he went and recruiting travelers. When the veteran trapper Milton Sublette saw the motley group at Elm Grove, he told White it was impossible to take a mixed party of 112 persons over the Trail and maintain harmony and discipline en route. White, prone to listen to no voice but his own, disagreed. He implied that his qualities as a leader would turn the trick.

At a meeting he was elected captain, and several resolutions were passed: "Every male of 18 years" should have a mule, horse, or wagon, a gun, three barrels of powder, one thousand caps or suitable flints, and fifty pounds of flour or meal, and thirty of bacon. A "scientific corps" of three would record everything concerning the road and journey that might be useful to the government and future emigrants. Also elected were a pilot (or scout), secretary, blacksmith, master wagonmaker, and even a master road and bridge builder. Every man, woman, and

Abandoned since the death of the fur trade, Astoria was drawn in 1841 by a U.S. Navy surgeon whose ship had sunk nearby. The flag was one of the few objects salvaged.

COLLECTION OF BRIG. GEN. PHILIP G. BLACKMORE

CITY ART MUSEUM OF ST. LOUIS

Albert Bierstadt's Nooning on the Platte *depicts the midday stop which rested men and oxen for the next push. The painting reflects a tranquility that was rare on the Trail.*

Marcus Whitman (on the white horse) sets out from Waiilatpu on his long and hazardous journey east to persuade church leaders to continue the Oregon missions.

child was registered, and no profane swearing was permitted at any time.

The train went into camp about four o'clock every afternoon. Every family had its own cookfire. Evenings were spent in visiting or singing. The women and children slept in the wagons; the men in tents or under the wagons. On clear nights the dogs howled at the moon and raced over the prairie. White did not like having his sleep disturbed; at the crossing of the Kansas River he ordered all dogs killed, giving as his excuse that their barking would alert the Indians farther out. Guns cracked, and some twenty dogs died. But then children howled, dog-loving men and women became infuriated, and the result was that Dr. White was instantly demoted and replaced by Lansford W. Hastings.

From that moment on, there was neither harmony nor discipline. The caravan split into small groups which traveled considerable distances apart to avoid one another's company. At Fort Laramie, White hired Thomas Fitzpatrick to pilot them to Oregon. The famous guide agreed, providing the wagon train tightened up. It did, though about half switched from wagons to pack mules. Heavy rainstorms and the Idaho desert caused the remaining wagons to be abandoned.

White and a few advance riders reached the Whitman mission first. They astounded the missionaries with news of the one hundred others toiling over the Trail not far behind. There is no record that Narcissa quailed at the thought of making one hundred unexpected guests comfortable. She and Marcus and their helpers rallied to the challenge. One of the emigrants wrote later, "Whitman has a very comfortable house and is farming to a considerable extent, has a threshing machine and grinding mill all under one roof drived by water power." And he spoke for everyone when he added, "I was never more pleased to see a house or white people in my life."

The emigrants moved on in a few days, leaving the mission yard littered and complaining bitterly at the prices Whitman asked for vegetables and flour produced by backbreaking toil in the Waiilatpu garden and mill. Ingratitude and garbage were not the only tokens of their passing. Dr. White delivered to Whitman a letter from the Mission Board. The directors wrote that they were sorry, but they could no longer maintain the expensive Oregon missions. Therefore, they were dismissing Henry Spalding, Asa Smith, and William Gray; whose complaints had irritated them. Worse, they ordered the Lapwai and Waiilatpu stations closed.

The letter was like a stab in the heart. Whitman dispatched Indian runners to bring in the other missionaries. After their emergency meeting, Whitman and A. L. Lovejoy set out at once for the East to plead their cause before the Board. The two rode off on fast horses. The threat of Sioux war parties in Idaho made them swing south into Colorado and New Mexico. Lovejoy's strength, severely taxed by snowstorms, frostbite, and starvation, failed him when they reached Bent's Fort, on the Arkansas River. He collapsed, but Whitman, his face mottled from frostbite, his lean frame wrapped in a buffalo coat, pushed on eastward.

In Washington he urged congressmen to establish more forts along the Oregon Trail for the protection of the emigrants. In New York City, he visited Horace Greeley and enlisted that great journalist's enthusiasm in the Oregon cause. Without changing his trail-soiled buckskins or visiting a barber, he laid his case before the complacent, humorless Mission Board. He persuaded them to rehire Spalding and to agree not to close Lapwai and Waiilatpu.

Whitman's eastbound winter ride across the mountains gave rise to the false legend that he had "saved" Oregon for the United States. Whitman never made such a claim, and many decades passed before the story was thoroughly disproved.

As Marcus Whitman hurried to Independence on his return trip, a flood tide was building. Men and women of unquenchable courage and spirit had marked out the trail to Oregon; the stage was set for the march to the Promised Land.

The Great Emigration of 1843 set in motion a tidal wave of westward-rolling pioneers. Describing the lure that drew them on, a woman wrote, "Oh, Oregon, you must be a wonderful country." This is Albert Bierstadt's idealized view of a caravan nearing the Promised Land.

BUTLER INSTITUTE OF AMERICAN ART

7.
The Great Emigration

The Great Emigration of 1843 was no spontaneous combustion. Several circumstances fueled this explosion of "Oregon fever." There was the hunger for land; the British threat to the Pacific Northwest; the aftereffects of the Panic of 1837; and equally important, the simple pioneering spirit of the American people.

The *Iowa Gazette* reported, "The Oregon fever is raging in almost every part of the Union. Companies are forming in the East, and in several parts of Ohio, which, added to those of Illinois, Iowa, and Missouri, will make a pretty formidable army.... It would be reasonable to suppose that there will be at least five thousand Americans west of the Rocky Mountains by next autumn."

When Marcus Whitman arrived in Independence, he was astonished at the number gathered there: "No less than 200 families, consisting of 1,000 persons of both sexes," and more than 120 wagons. Since Oregon was rumored to be a stockman's paradise, some 3,500 head of cattle had been collected for the trip west.

This was a far cry from the ten-wagon Smith, Jackson, and Sublette caravan of 1830. These bright wagons were giant-wheeled and overloaded with furniture, plows, churns, and nonessentials. The roster included scores of women and children, dogs, cats, chickens, and an occasional bird in a cage. Smith's men were familiar with the Trail and knew its dangers; these 1843 travelers were real tenderfeet.

Independence was exciting, odorous, and dusty. The crude hotels and taverns were jammed; the wheelwrights', wagonmakers', and outfitters' shops crowded; the streets choked with traffic; the outskirts swarming with tents. Here, too, the Santa Fe traders purchased mules from the largest mule market on the continent and packed their freight wagons. Steamboats unloaded tons of supplies and hundreds of emigrants. Everyone, save the merchants, was on the move. As soon as a wagon was loaded, it was moved to the rendezvous encampments on the prairie, remaining there until departure day.

On May 22, this advance guard of the Great Emigration of 1843 pulled out of Elm Grove. For four days and forty miles the ponderous column traveled the Santa Fe Trail. At present-day Gardner, Kansas, those "for Oregon" turned northwest. They left leafy trees and farmed acres behind.

Soon they saw their first Indians—ninety Kansas and Osage warriors mounted on prancing ponies, bearing lances, shields, and bows, their faces painted vermilion and their dark hair bristling with feathers. The men readied guns, the women clutched babies, and the children hid under quilts, though they need not. These and other Indians encountered throughout the journey would stare insolently, steal a few horses, sometimes threaten, but otherwise let them pass unharmed. Later travelers were not so fortunate.

Pandemonium reigned during this

MISSOURI HISTORICAL SOCIETY

For reasons of health, age, or lack of capital, not everyone could seek a new life beyond the Rockies. In this painting a family bound for Oregon bids a tearful farewell to relatives.

Once on the Trail, pioneers had to forget the amenities of life back east. These camp scenes were sketched by twenty-three-year-old William Henry Jackson. Above, men cook over a buffalo-chip fire, using long-handled implements to avoid the searing heat. Below, a reluctant ox struggles to evade the yoke.

brief shakedown ride. Drivers fought for places up front out of the dust; others raced their wagons over the prairie to be first at the wood and water of the campsites. Those who did not own cattle refused to stand night guard over the herd and complained because the cattle held the road speed to a slow drag. They hankered for a fast trip to the Promised Land, unmindful of what speed would do to their wagons, to their oxen, and to themselves.

Fortunately, more sober-minded men prevailed. After the party ferried across the Kansas River, officers were elected. Missourian Peter Burnett was chosen captain and a "Council of Ten" elected in a novel manner: candidates for the council lined up and walked across the grass, their supporters "balloting" by falling in behind their man.

Rules of conduct and travel were agreed upon, and the wagons were inspected. The huge, unruly caravan was divided into a lighter column consisting of sixty-one wagons, unencumbered by cattle, and a "cow column" of almost equal strength made up of the stock owners, their families, wagons, and animals. A cool, thoughtful farmer from Missouri, Jesse Applegate, proved a most fortunate choice for leader of this column, and his lively account, *A Day with the Cow Column*, is a superb record of covered wagon travel. Both divisions kept within supporting distance of each other on the excellent road to the Platte.

Applegate wrote that Whitman's "great experience and indomitable energy were of priceless value to the migrating column. His constant advice was, 'Travel, travel, travel; nothing else will take you to the end of your journey; nothing is wise that does not help you along; nothing is good for you that causes a moment's delay.'"

This challenge to keep moving despite weather, sickness, and human procrastination tested Applegate severely. Fortunately, he failed neither himself nor his followers. Before the stars dimmed, his sentries roused the camp. While smoke from the breakfast fires spiraled skyward, sixty men rounded up the stock and yoked the oxen. Sleepy children toted water and milked family cows. Wives cooked sowbelly (bacon) and slam-johns (flapjacks). Families ate at portable tables, on the ground, or standing up. As the sky dappled pink and yellow and the sun rose quickly in pale spring radiance, bugles drowned out the larks' piping, and the wagons began to roll.

Applegate divided the cow column into four platoons, which often moved abreast across the broad grassland. Those in the lead one day dropped to the rear the next; thus no one could complain about position. The dawdlers either kept moving or ate dust.

Night guard was essential—a lonely, spooky vigil under a vast, star-studded sky, the immense quiet broken only by wolves' howling. The lightning and rainstorms seemed worse than any they had encountered before. Several mornings they started out in a downpour without breakfast, the men sloshing in knee-deep mud, the wheels slewing, the livestock skittish. The wise kept dry kindling under canvas so that when the sky cleared there could be quick fires. Wagons, and the ropes strung between them, bloomed with drying clothing and quilts.

Kansas' rolling hills were ablaze with wild flowers, and scarcely a person or ox lacked a posy. The journey up the valley of the Little Blue would always be recalled with joy. As they crossed into present-day Nebraska they began to see buffalo tracks and wallows and prairie dog villages that delighted the children. By now all but the infants and the elderly were walking. The train averaged from twelve to fifteen miles daily.

The Platte River, handsome from afar, was so muddy that some claimed it flowed "bottom-side up." Here the

Meetings with veteran trappers like the one in this contemporary painting helped tenderfoot emigrants learn of the dangers ahead.

emigrants turned their backs on the prairie and entered the immense, thin-soiled grassy plains. Except for cottonwoods and willows on islands in the river, the land was almost wholly devoid of trees. With no wood or even twigs for cookfires, the emigrants gathered large gray chips of dried buffalo dung for fuel, making their fires in small trenches so that the flaming embers would not scatter in the constant wind. Not until the wagons circled at Cottonwood Spring was there clear water and scrub cedar for firewood. The spring was the scene of wholesale laundering.

By this time even the puny found their appetites whetted by the invigorating exercise and the open-fire cooking. Antelope steaks proved more succulent than veal, and prairie-chicken stew spiced with sage powdered between the fingers was a new treat. As a fiddler scraped his violin, or the reedy notes of a mouth organ floated over the night air, babies and toddlers were hustled to bed, kettles scoured, and bean pots buried in hot coals to cook savoringly overnight. The young people began dancing and singing; the women gossiped; the men bragged about their future plans. In an hour or so the music stilled, and all but the guards bedded down.

Afternoons were warm going up the Platte. The slow pace and monotonous country brought on midday drowsiness until one day a man shouted, "Buffalo!"

Men and boys jerked their guns from saddle slings and slammed their heels into their horses' ribs. Yelling like Indians, they rode pell-mell down on the dark herd. The animals bolted. In the thickening dust, bulls and cows bawled, shots rang out, huge beasts turned nose over tail—and some riders, too. By a miracle the only casualties were buffalo. That night the air was full of the aroma of roasting and frying ribs and tongues. Young lads scorned table sitting, and mountain man fashion, hunkered down on their heels to eat the big ribs.

The column made its way to the forks of the Platte and then continued up the South Platte for about sixty miles before crossing. The wagon beds were waterproofed with green buffalo hides, and double and triple teams were chained on to cross the swift stream.

The wagons continued up the south bank of the North Platte. The road was climbing now, and the going became rougher. The happy mood of the Kansas prairies evaporated as humans and animals plodded along, and tempers became short. Fort Laramie was a godsend. Everyone rested, wagons were repaired, and food stocks replenished. They had covered 667 miles in forty days, but soon it was time to move on.

On July 14 a dust cloud suggested more buffalo. But the shadows shaped into ponies, and the flickering colors became the lance pennants and headdresses of a long line of Cheyennes who, in Applegate's words, "made a most proud appearance."

Whitman kept urging, "Travel, travel, travel": travel over swift rivers, then dry out; travel through sandy, deep-gullied hills; flounder over the North Platte crossing 127 miles beyond Fort Laramie; mix grease and gunpowder to paint names and dates and "The Oregon Company arrived July 26, 1843" on Independence Rock. They rolled through strangling dust, parching wind, a purgatory of insects, and on over South Pass; they were 947 miles out now, about halfway to the Columbia. They pushed across the dry sage plain to the far side of the Green, traveling at night to avoid the broiling sun. Creaking and lurching to the top of a mountainous divide, they collapsed in the thick grass along the Bear River. The oxen must rest! Humans, too.

The lush Bear Meadows, near what is now Montpelier, Idaho, deserve much credit for the success of this and later Oregon migrations. Without this lifesaving respite, American westering might well have stopped short against an insurmountable barrier of exhaustion and mounting hunger. The good water, trout and wild fowl, elk, wild onions, berries, and knee-high grass of this oasis in an otherwise harsh land recharged energies and spirits.

The bubbling waters of Soda Springs, Steamboat Springs, and Beer Spring delighted everyone. But when they reached Fort Hall on the Snake River, half the families were facing starvation. Thinking about the bacon rinds, leftover biscuits, and buffalo meat discarded along the Trail, or the furniture chopped up for firewood, or the plows and chests abandoned to lighten the load, left a deep scar on adult memories. Worse, the trading post man told them they could not go beyond Fort Hall with their wagons.

Despair seized many. If they abandoned the wagons, there were not horses or mules enough to carry them forward. They sought out Whitman. He assured them that the wagons could get through the remaining 650 miles to the Columbia because there were strong backs and tools enough to clear the way. When the pilot and some twenty others turned south toward California, the company offered Whitman four hundred dollars to lead the way to Oregon. He accepted readily.

Axletrees shattered and wagons tipped over on rocks and three-foot-high clumps of sagebrush. The jagged path gashed the feet of the oxen, marking the trail in blood. Still they pushed on. It took forty men wielding axes four days to open the way over the Blue Mountains. At some points they had to lower the wagons by ropes down the rocky slopes. A snowfall seemed a disaster, but it melted quickly.

Finally the worst was over. Frost ripened the berries, and the emigrants feasted. Fresh vegetables were available for a stiff price at the mission on the Umatilla River and again at Waiilatpu. On October 16, 1843, twenty-one adventuresome, wearying weeks and over 1,800 miles from Independence, the wagons halted at Fort Walla Walla, near the Columbia River. The overland trek was behind them.

From Fort Walla Walla or The Dalles, the horde of land seekers sought river transportation. On arriving in the Willamette Valley, the nearly nine hundred newcomers found the beginnings of local civil government already established. The sound of axes rang out across the valley as claims were cleared. One of the emigrants ended his travel diary with these two entries:

"Friday, October 27.—Arrived at Oregon City at the Falls of the Willamette.

"Saturday, October 28.—Went to work."

Silhouetted by the ghostly moonlight of the plains, the sentinel in Frederic Remington's painting stands with his rifle cocked, listening for the slightest sound of marauding Indians or stampeding buffalo. At nightfall the wagons were parked in a circle for added safety.

DENVER PUBLIC LIBRARY WESTERN COLLECTION

The pioneers staring out of this superb old photograph reflect in their faces the hardships of trail life and, above all, a grim determination to reach their goal.

California was a land of milk and honey, according to reports that filtered back to poor or bankrupted eastern farmers. But, as this painting shows, the parched Nevada wasteland exacted a terrible toll on settlers trying to reach the valleys of the new Promised Land.

STANFORD UNIVERSITY MUSEUM

8.
Frontier on the Pacific

Oregon was not the only goal of the thousands who guided their wagons westward across the prairies and mountains. Twelve hundred miles out from Independence the Oregon Trail forked — those for Oregon went right; those who sought California turned left.

The earliest known route blazed from the vicinity of the Oregon Trail to California was that of the incomparable Jedediah Smith. In 1826, he and fourteen men explored for beaver southward from Soda Springs, down the east side of Great Salt Lake and the Utah Valley, and on to the Beaver and Colorado rivers. They struggled across the Mojave Desert and finally reached California.

Returning by a more northerly route, Smith and two companions were the first white men to cross the Sierra Nevada range, emerging south of Walker Lake. They had to stumble on foot across the dreary wastelands of Nevada to reach the fur rendezvous at Bear Lake, Utah, on July 1, 1827.

In spite of the countless terrifying experiences of his journey, Smith set out again just ten days later for California. As before, he missed finding the Humboldt River route, which was to become the standard trail for California-bound emigrants. This time Smith pushed all the way up the Pacific coast before returning to the Rockies via Fort Vancouver and the Columbia; twice he narrowly escaped Indian attacks which killed twenty-five of his men.

Although Smith and his expedition clerk left fairly adequate accounts and provided information for a map of these grand-loop journeys, Smith's trail was soon forgotten. This remarkable pathfinder, who might well have become a greater emigrant guide than even Tom Fitzpatrick, Jim Bridger, or Kit Carson, was killed by Comanches on the Santa Fe Trail in 1831.

Now Captain Bonneville and his scout, Joseph Reddeford Walker, came on the scene. In 1833 Bonneville dispatched Walker and a fur brigade to investigate the beaver potential of the region between the Rockies and California. They moved southwest of the Great Salt Lake, but by a more northerly route than Jed Smith had followed. Crossing arid Nevada and topping the Sierras was a rugged bout for even these tough mountain men. On the summit they floundered amidst huge boulders, rock slides, snowbanks, and stunted trees. In trying to locate a descent, Walker led them southward along the broad summit and thus earned the distinction for his party of being the first whites to look down on Yosemite Valley.

Backtracking, Walker eventually found an Indian pass down to the San Joaquin Valley. After lowering their horses over a succession of vertical cliffs, they came to some "trees of the Redwood species, incredibly large" — the Merced or Tuolumne groves of giant Sequoias.

Again, time and weather wiped out Walker's trail, and so the next expedition to turn off the Oregon Trail to reach California had to blaze its own way. This was the Bidwell-Bartleson party.

In 1839 young John Bidwell developed a bad case of "California fever." This Missouri teacher-farmer was infected by one of the far-ranging Robidoux brothers, newly returned from the Pacific with tales of sunshine, easy living, and a land far richer than foggy, rain-drenched Oregon. Bidwell became so excited that he invited his neighbors to hear Robidoux. They, too, caught the fever and spread it far. The result was the formation of the Western Emigration Society, which enrolled over five hundred enthusiastic members. Since most of them were poor folk who needed time to scrape together the barest of essentials for the journey, they agreed to rendezvous at Sapling Grove, near Independence, early in May of 1841.

The local merchants, alarmed at this threatened exodus of patrons, spoke of California with great scorn. In the spring of 1841 copies of a letter written by the disillusioned Thomas J.

Jedediah Smith's band of trappers labors across the Mojave Desert in 1826. The determined Smith first proved that an overland trip to California was possible.

Mules became particularly stubborn and ornery as desert temperatures soared to well over a hundred degrees. The men above, coaxing their animals forward in the shimmering heat, approach Death Valley. The party below, sketched in 1849, threads its way down a steep mountain slope east of Great Salt Lake. Often, wagons had to be lowered by ropes.

Farnham were widely circulated. Farnham had been one of the ill-fated Oregon Dragoons of 1839; when his harrowing account got around, the Western Emigration Society fell apart.

However, Bidwell could not be dissuaded. He arrived at Sapling Grove, and others straggled in until the company consisted of sixty-nine men, women, and children.

John Bartleson was elected captain, but only because he threatened to withdraw himself and eight husky companions if he were not chosen. The members were so poor that Bidwell doubted if there was a hundred dollars in cash among them all. They were impatient to start, but as Bidwell wrote later, "No one knew where to go, not even the captain."

Fortunately the great Thomas Fitzpatrick was just ahead on the Trail, leading some Catholic missionaries to the Flathead nation in Montana. This group included Father Pierre Jean de Smet, Father Gregory Mengarini, and ten French Canadians who transported their belongings in squeaky, two-wheeled Red River carts, each drawn by a pair of mules. Fitzpatrick agreed that the Bidwell-Bartleson party might tag along, though he must have looked askance at their inadequacies.

At first one day was much like another. The men hunted antelope, prairie wolves, and buffalo. Bidwell wrote of the buffalo, "One night when we were encamped on the South Fork of the Platte, they came in such droves that we had to sit up and make what fires we could to keep them from running over us. . . . We could hear them thundering all night long; the ground fairly trembled with vast approaching bands." A few days later a terrible rainstorm, followed by four inches of hail, forced the train to stop. When a whirling waterspout passed only a quarter of a mile away, the men braced themselves against the wagons to keep them from being bowled over.

One of Bidwell's friends, Nicholas Dawson, rode too far from the company and suddenly saw a band of Cheyennes riding down on him. With a spear at his back, he was forced to yield his knife, gun, and clothing. When the Indians raced away, Dawson returned to the train. Swearing vengeance, he dressed hastily, borrowed a horse and gun, and left "to give them battle." Fortunately Fitzpatrick stopped him with some forcible language and powwowed with the thieves. By offering substitute gifts and smoking the peace pipe, he retrieved Dawson's belongings. After that the company dubbed the young man "Cheyenne" Dawson.

At Soda Springs, Fitzpatrick and the priests turned north. On comparing notes, the Bidwell-Bartleson men discovered that they "only knew that California lay to the west." Understandably, half of them decided not to venture into the trackless expanse and continued on the route to Oregon.

The remainder, including Mr. and Mrs. Benjamin Kelsey and their infant daughter, "took the left-hand road to

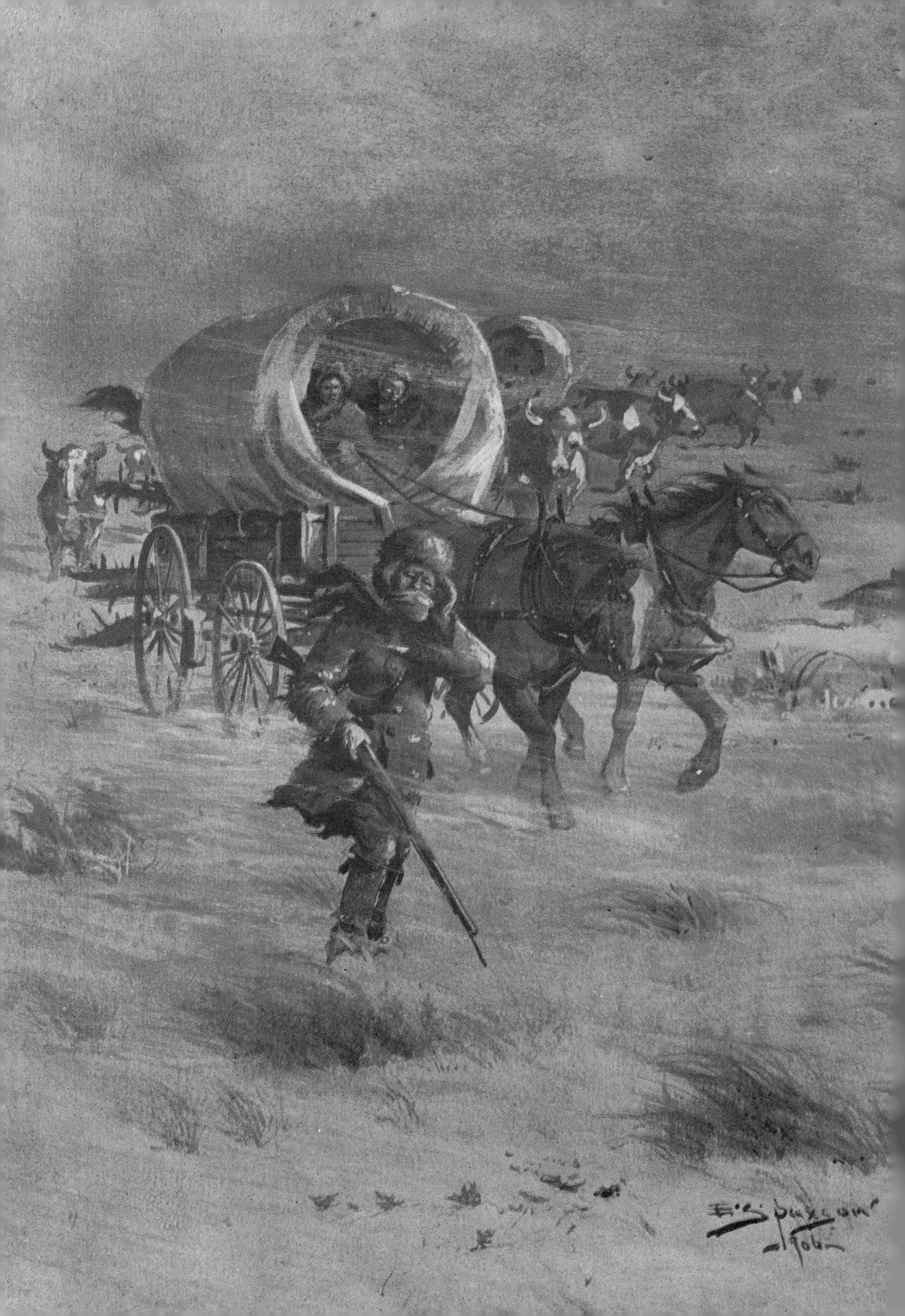

California." There was no road, only the faintest trappers' trail down the west side of the Bear River. The days were hot, the nights freezing. September forest fires obscured the valley of the Great Salt Lake. This country was thick with sagebrush tough enough to overturn a light wagon. But the hares and sage hens that took shelter under the scraggly growth provided welcome meat, and when gathered in quantities, sagebrush made a hot, bright fire.

By September 16 the wagons had to be abandoned (five years later another party used them for firewood). Then game became scarce, and water and grass infrequent. They traveled too far south, but stumbled on to the South Fork of the Humboldt, following it to the main stream. Farther along they ran into the vast tule marshes bordering Carson Sink.

Somehow the company managed twenty miles daily, although the traveling was pure misery. When starvation threatened, they butchered a poor ox. Bidwell's account, like many others', shows how badly most felt for their patient, exhausted animals, how they struggled to feed and water them, and how they wept unashamedly when the oxen dropped in their yokes. At last they came to the Stanislaus River and followed it to the San Joaquin Valley.

In 1844 white-bearded Elisha Stevens (right) captained the first wagon train that reached California. Two years later the Donner-Reed party was trapped in the Sierras by a howling blizzard like the one at the left.

Mrs. Kelsey and her baby were the first woman and child to cross overland to California by way of the Great Salt Lake-Humboldt-Sierra Nevada route. The hardships did not dampen Bidwell's enthusiasm, nor did California disappoint him. His diary, printed in 1842, encouraged others to journey to the rainbow's end.

Some 1,400 pilgrims reached Oregon in 1844 via the Oregon Trail; the same year, the first wagons turned off to California and topped the Sierras. This was the Stevens-Townsend-Murphy party, guided by eighty-one-year-old Caleb Greenwood.

Deep snow near present Donner Lake forced temporary abandonment of the wagons. Seventeen-year-old Moses Schallenberger volunteered to stay behind and guard them because he "did not suppose that the snow would at any time be more than two feet deep, or that it would be on the ground continually."

Joseph Foster and Allen Montgomery agreed to stay with him. After leaving them two poor cows, the main party trudged on foot to Sutter's Fort. Schallenberger, Foster, and Montgomery raised a cabin as snow piled three feet on the level. They could not hunt, so they butchered the cows. Fortunately there was plenty of firewood at hand. It continued snowing so heavily that by December the men feared they would be buried alive.

They decided to fashion crude snowshoes and shoulder packs and to try to cross the summit. But one grueling day's travel exhausted Moses, and he returned to the cabin alone. Foster and Montgomery pushed on, and being sturdier, completed their journey.

When weather permitted, Schallenberger hunted and trapped. He roasted coyote meat in a Dutch oven. It was terrible, and it was just as bad when he boiled it. Then he roasted a fat fox he had trapped, which proved to be delicious. He had plenty of books, borrowed from one of the wagons, and read aloud to break the maddening stillness. This persisted until the end of February, when a rescuer reached him with provisions. In the spring, the wagons were brought the final rugged miles across the hump and into California.

Disaster rode with another large expedition that departed from Independence in May of 1846. This company, organized at Springfield, Illinois, by the Donner and Reed families, fared well as far as Fort Bridger. But the men had heard about the Hastings' Cutoff, a short cut around the southern end of Great Salt Lake and across the Utah-Nevada desert to California. James Clyman, guiding another party, had traveled the route earlier with trappers and advised strongly against it. Nevertheless, the Donners, the Reeds, and others, numbering eighty-seven men, women, and children, decided to chance it.

At first the trail was "all that could be desired." It was tough going in Echo Canyon, but then they dropped down to the grassy Great Salt Lake Valley and had no difficulty in pulling around the south shore of the lake. After refreshing themselves at the springs in the Tooele Valley, they set out for Pilot Peak a hundred miles away.

The August sun beating down on white salt flats dehydrated humans and animals. Used to rattlesnakes, now they faced the new threat of scorpions. Along the Humboldt River and Carson Sink the passage was strewn with the carcasses of their expired livestock. Nights were hideous, as wolves howled and fought over the meat. Then the fertile Truckee Meadows proved a lifesaving boon. Their skin and clothes

Enraged by an epidemic that he thought was a white man's plot, the Cayuse brave Tamahas cut down Marcus Whitman and helped kill eleven others. Tamahas' face was "the most savage I ever beheld," said the artist.

stiff with sweat and dirt, entire families waded into the cool, clear water, soaking away grime and fatigue, and discouragement, too. Cattle fed to the bursting point and rested.

They could have used a month to recuperate before tackling the abrupt, timber- and boulder-strewn east slope of the Sierra Nevadas. But delays had already split the Donner-Reed group, with the five Donner wagons dropping behind. The advancing season became their enemy now. Beyond the Little Truckee River the advance guard of the main company became alarmed. Pointing to the stormy sky, the leaders urged the utmost haste in crossing the range. They moved on, and near Truckee Lake (now Donner Lake), they saw snowflakes "as large as saucers." Though they camped in the snow, they made it safely to the warm valley at the foot of the Pacific slope.

On October 28 the main body of the company reached Truckee Lake and, for two bitter days, bucked five feet of soft snow. When a fresh storm buffeted them, they knew the worst: they were trapped. The men chipped weakly at logs and somehow raised two cabins. They repaired the Schallenberger cabin a quarter of a mile from the lake.

To the rear the five wagons of the Donner group were in even greater jeopardy. Though the men tried, they lacked the strength to fell logs for cabins, and so tents were fortified with branches and blankets. These were soon buried under fourteen feet of snow. The livestock froze in the forty-foot drifts. Silently, dreadfully, the snow continued to fall.

For weeks the stranded emigrants of the two parties suffered unspeakable hardships, and ultimately they were forced to eat the flesh of dead comrades in order to survive. Of fifteen who braved starvation and agonizing frostbite for twenty-five days in December and January in a valiant effort to summon help, eight died on the way. Relief parties reached the snowbound emigrants in February and March. Of the original eighty-seven, only forty-five survived this terrible page in the history of American overland migration.

Today the cabin sites are well marked,

and bronze figures set atop a stone pedestal twenty-two feet high—the depth of the snow that winter of 1846—remind twentieth-century travelers riding swiftly and smoothly over a modern highway of the toll wreaked on some who dared move west.

This tragedy did not deter others from moving overland to California. A trickle of wagons continued to turn off at Soda Springs or Fort Hall and make safe passage to the Golden Gate. But until 1849 the bulk of the traffic on the Oregon Trail carried on to Oregon, either on the old road or on a newer route across northern California and thence northward to Oregon.

Nearly 5,000 in five companies emigrated to Oregon in 1845, and in the next year, while an estimated 1,350 Oregon-bound emigrants were on the Trail, the Oregon country officially became part of the United States.

It is probably fair to say that the Great Emigration of 1843, as one historian puts it, "clinched the argument for the United States" when the British and Americans reopened negotiations in 1846. The British had become alarmed over the heat generated by the "Oregon question" during the presidential campaign of 1844. Their concern deepened on reading President James Polk's inaugural address, which hinted strongly that the United States just might take a huge bite out of Britain's Pacific Northwest colony.

So both sides compromised. The boundary agreed upon was the 49th parallel, with Vancouver Island remaining British. The treaty was approved by the United States Senate on June 15, 1846. At long last, the "Oregon question" was settled.

That same year the great American historian Francis Parkman rode from Independence to Fort Laramie, keeping a daily diary; thereafter he wrote probably the most widely-read book on the Oregon Trail, brilliantly recording the sight and sound and feel of the journey. He saw "tall, awkward men in brown homespun" and bone-weary women "with cadaverous faces and long lank figures." Though so ill at times that he could scarcely sit his horse, Parkman wove an unforgettable tapestry in prose. Reading *The Oregon Trail* is second only to traveling the Trail itself.

The feverish missionary impulse had about burned itself out by this time. As homeseekers crowded the roads west (4,500 arrived in Oregon in 1847 alone), support for converting the heathen dwindled. Jason Lee was dismissed from the mission service, and the great dream of Methodist expansion dribbled out. Many missions closed as the Indians became increasingly hostile to the white hordes taking over their land.

The Presbyterians and Congregationalists also dropped their costly outposts, and Marcus Whitman soon found himself limited to farming and doctoring. When the Cayuse tribe contracted measles from passing emigrants, more than half of them succumbed. Rumor convinced the survivors that the sickness was a white man's plot to kill them all. They forgot the kindness and the ministering. On the pretense of seeking help, a number of braves entered Whitman's mission on November 29, 1847, and killed Marcus, Narcissa, and ten others.

When word reached the Willamette Valley, the settlers raised an army of volunteers who attacked the Cayuse and drove them out of their country. They also sent mountain man Joe Meek (whose daughter had died in the Whitman massacre) streaking across the continent with the tragic news and a demand that Congress do something about Oregon.

Both Meek and Oregon profited from that ride. On August 14, 1848, Congress passed a bill creating the Territory of Oregon. Territorial government was set up in March of 1849, with General Joseph Lane as Oregon's first governor, and Meek, the one-time trapper, as United States marshal. He swapped his loose-fitting buckskins, symbol of freedom and frontiering, for the more prosaic, tight-fitting frock coat of officialdom.

This drawing shows the suddenness and savagery of the attack on the unsuspecting Whitman mission. Actually, Narcissa was in another room when Marcus was killed.

Fleeing from religious bigotry and violence, the vanguard of the Mormon exodus of 1847 descends into their newfound Zion. Questioned on the decision to settle in the arid Great Salt Lake Valley, Mormon leader Brigham Young replied, "God has made the choice."

COLLECTION OF HOWARD R. DRIGGS.

9.
The Mormon Trek

In the year 1847 the Oregon Trail became a roadway of sorrow and hope for a religious sect seeking a haven from persecution and mob violence.

The adherents of the Mormon faith had experienced ever-increasing hostility since their founder, Joseph Smith, organized the Mormon Church at Fayette, New York, in 1830. Known officially as the Church of Jesus Christ of Latter-Day Saints, the members accepted, in addition to the Bible, the Book of Mormon. This consisted of sacred writings, which Smith said were revealed to him in a vision and which he found in the form of golden tablets near Palmyra, New York, translated, and published.

The Mormons kept to themselves, considering all others nonbelievers, and this made their neighbors angry and suspicious. Hoping to find an area far removed from such hostility, where they could live and practice their beliefs in freedom and peace, Joseph Smith and the Mormons moved west, first to Ohio, then to Missouri, and finally to the Illinois frontier. But many others also sought this rich prairie land, and before long the hard-working Mormons found themselves subject to mounting harassment.

To make matters worse, Smith caused a national uproar by approving the practice of polygamy—allowing a man to have more than one wife—for leaders of the church. Violence was now inevitable. In June of 1844, at Carthage, Illinois, Joseph Smith and his brother Hyrum were murdered by those who thought, mistakenly, that killing the leaders would bring about the collapse of the church. Instead, a stronger man took command—Brigham Young.

An uneasy peace between Mormons and Gentiles (as they called nonbelievers) existed until September, 1845, when over 150 Mormon dwellings at Lima, Illinois, were burned and the inhabitants driven off their property. Conditions worsened steadily. Finally, in February, 1846, Brigham Young and some 2,000 of his followers fled in sub-zero weather across the frozen Mississippi River.

Though their suffering was intense, and many perished, Young pushed on across southern Iowa. Soon there was a steady stream of wagons on the move. To provision the near-destitute, Young ordered his advance party to break ground at each campsite. The next arrivals planted seed; later ones weeded and irrigated; and the late summer parties harvested the crops and transported them to winter quarters across the Missouri at what is now Omaha, Nebraska.

As more and more Gentiles settled near their winter quarters, Young looked farther westward. He and his advisers read avidly the reports of Lt. John Charles Frémont. In 1842 and 1843 Frémont had led official government explorations of much of the Oregon Trail, the Great Salt Lake Valley, Oregon, and California. The glowing enthusiasm of Frémont's report, backed by detailed information on the Trail, terrain, soil, weather, plants, and locations for military posts, had added fresh fuel to the national excitement over California and the Oregon country.

Dashing, charming, well-schooled in scientific observation, Frémont was eager to find fame in the West. With the help of his brilliant wife Jessie and his politically powerful father-in-law, Missouri Senator Thomas Hart Benton, Frémont was chosen to provide a guidebook for the emigrants who would be encouraged to settle in Oregon and wrest it from British control.

Wisely selecting Kit Carson as his guide and pathfinder, Frémont's explorations were highly successful, and the fame he sought was his.

Thanks to the reports of Frémont and others, Brigham Young decided on the location for his proposed Kingdom of the Saints. It was not California or Oregon, but the vast valley of the Great Salt Lake. At the time, this was Mexican territory. Young concluded that it would remain so and thus afford the freedom from persecution the Mormons had sought in vain on American soil.

Joseph Smith, Mormonism's founder, and his brother were murdered in an Illinois jail by a mob. Here a masked killer is prevented from mutilating Smith's body.

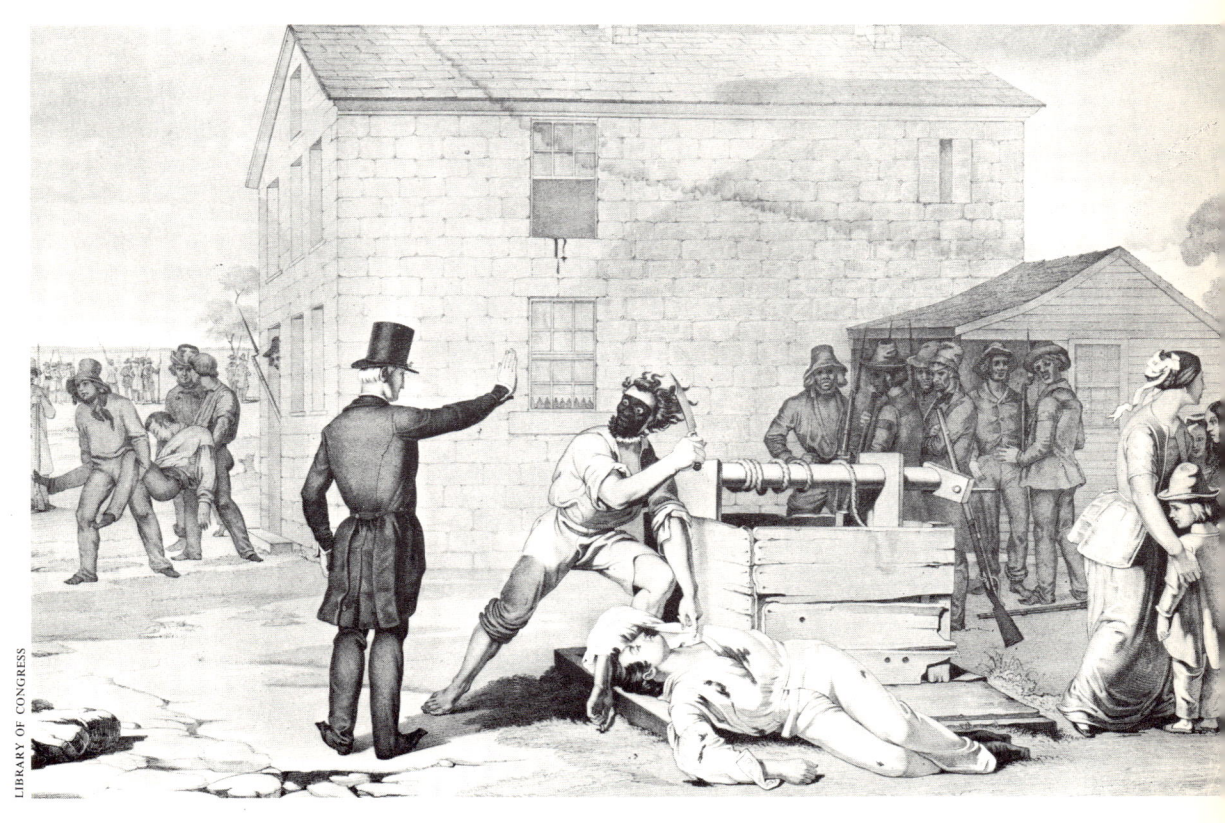

111

On April 9, 1847, the Mormon vanguard, or Pioneers as they called themselves, moved out on the Oregon Trail — seventy-three wagons, 143 men and boys, three women and two infants, plus horses, mules, oxen, chickens, and seventeen dogs. The men were divided into companies of one hundred, fifty, and ten, with captains over each. All were armed, and a cannon was dragged along "to overawe hostile Indians." The wagons creaked under the weight of plows and other implements, seed grain, and a year's supply of provisions.

Bugle call at 5 A.M. roused the company. After breakfast and prayers, the wagons moved out in close file, sometimes five abreast. Scouts and hunters rode in advance, with Young at the head of the column. The remaining men walked with rifles readied for defense against Gentiles as well as Indians. William Clayton, the official diarist, remarked of the early part of the journey, "The roads are very good." The wagons circled at night, the animals were pastured inside, and after prayers all but the guards were in bed by 9 P.M.

In mid-May buffalo herds crossing the Trail were so vast, numbering hundreds of thousands, that the pace slowed, and at times, halted. Young forbade wholesale slaughter of the beasts, not only because he disapproved of wastefulness, but so that an adequate meat supply remained for those companies to follow.

The Pioneers withstood the expected torment of rain, mud, insects, and dust. Most of them suffered from dysentery and bad water; a few were treated for rattlesnake bites. When a little girl slipped beneath a wagon and a wheel rolled over her leg, it was treated with oil of camphor and prayer. Cannon fire kept pilfering Indians at a safe distance.

To avoid other emigrant parties, the Pioneers broke new ground that eventually became known as the Mormon Trail. Instead of following the south bank of the Platte as had earlier Oregon-bound settlers, the Mormons blazed a new road north of the river. To guide future companies they even established a communications system by nailing signboards to fifteen-foot poles set alongside the road.

Poor Scribe Clayton! One of his tasks was to compute the daily mileage by counting every wheel revolution on his wagon. Small wonder that by the time Fort Laramie was in sight he complained of eye fatigue. After that, an ingenious mechanism of wooden cogs was used to measure distance.

The Pioneers crossed to the south side of the Platte to obtain provisions at Fort Laramie and to await others of the brethren. When they did not arrive by June 4, Young gave orders to move ahead, leaving the following note: "If experience has not already taught you, we would say, keep a sharp lookout for buffalo, Indians, and bears."

At the end of every day's journey, Clayton had mileage posts and direction signs erected while others checked

Strong-willed Brigham Young steered his followers "up into the mountains, where the devil cannot dig us out." Without his guidance the Mormon Church might have perished.

the Frémont guidebook to make sure they were on the right track. Where the Oregon Trail crossed the North Platte, the river was in flood. "After confabulating for a half hour," the Pioneers emptied their wagons and floated their goods across on a leather-bottomed "skift." A large party of Oregon-bound settlers arrived and offered to pay a dollar and a half per wagon if the Mormons would ferry them over. Since the "year's provisions" had dwindled alarmingly, Young chose to accept payment in flour, bacon, and meal. He left ten young men to continue ferry operations and bring desperately needed funds into the church coffer.

Moving up the Sweetwater, the column detoured around a heavy bank of snow, and grown men joined young boys in a snowball fight. At South Pass they encountered eastbound traders. The march halted while they exchanged news and swapped Eastern newspapers for Oregon and California papers. With typical greenhorn enthusiasm, the sober Mormons bought the traders' leftover stock of buckskin pants and shirts, much to Young's dismay.

Beyond the Green River, Oregon-bound companies turned northwest toward Fort Hall. Clayton dutifully reported, "We took the left-hand road which leads to California."

On July 7 and 8 the Pioneers rested at Fort Bridger, the trading post that Jim Bridger had established in 1842 on Black's Fork of the Green River. "How much farther is the Great Salt Lake?" they asked Bridger. He thought it was about one hundred miles, more or less. Hurrah!

Their joy evaporated as they struggled over an ever-worsening trail. Men and animals neared exhaustion; wagons fell apart in spite of constant care. Overexertion and insufficient food made many ill, and even Brigham Young was prostrated with fever. On July 19 the precipitous cliffs along the Weber River stopped them.

Young dispatched Orson Pratt with a party to locate a trail and improve the worst spots. After several disappointing tries, the young men found a way. They labored hard, inspired by the knowledge that they were but a

CHURCH OF JESUS CHRIST OF LATTER-DAY SAINTS

Women and children gather buffalo chips and light fires as the rest of a Mormon hand-cart brigade, painted by a fellow settler, trudges into camp during the trek westward.

few miles short of the Kingdom. One of them reported to Young, "We have opened a road thru the kanyon where it is uncertain whether man or beast ever trod before unless it be a bear or a rattlesnake." On July 22 Pratt and his companions dropped their tools and bedrolls on the long-sought site.

Two days later Brigham Young raised from his bed in Heber Kimball's wagon, lifted the wagon sheet, and viewed from a high point the broad green valley. It was ribboned with creeks and ringed with foothills and mountains. The lake and the great barren salt flats shimmered in the brilliant sunshine. Legend has Young saying, "This is the place. Drive on."

The wagons rolled down into four-foot-high grass on the bottom land. Pratt's men had already turned the sod, planted seed potatoes and grain, and diverted water from a stream, beginning a network of irrigation canals that eventually transformed the semidesert into a bountiful harvest land.

In the next few days a site was stepped off for a temple and a city two miles square was laid out. In present-day Pioneer Square the first adobe-and-log houses were raised as part of a fort. Young sent others to explore the settlement possibilities of the Bear River Valley, Cache Valley, and Utah Valley. They were to locate

Having fulfilled the vision of Joseph Smith and Brigham Young, this Mormon emigrant poses with his family, secure at last in a land far removed from persecution.

UNION PACIFIC RAILROAD

timber, dam and mill sites, and to plant orchards, potatoes, and grain.

Young and the Mormons thought themselves a safe thousand miles from their enemies. But they were to be bitterly disappointed when, after the Mexican War, the territory was ceded to the United States. The Mormons were once more part of the nation they had fled. Even when Salt Lake City swarmed with gold stampeders in 1849, the Mormons largely obeyed Young's orders to remain aloof socially, though the brethren might carry on a profitable business with the travelers.

Not long after Young and the Pioneers had arrived, reports came in that nine companies were crossing the plains, totaling more than four hundred families with 566 wagons and over 5,000 head of livestock. On September 9, 1847, Young penned words that hold true to this day: "We have fulfilled the mission . . . by selecting and pointing out to you a beautiful site for a city, which is destined to be a place of refuge for the oppressed, and one that is calculated to please the eye, to cheer the heart, and fill the hungry soul with food."

The following year, 1848, the Oregon Trail was all but monopolized by Mormons emigrating to their Promised Land. In the following eight years nearly 60,000 Mormons traveled the Trail. There were many European converts who could not afford ship passage, wagons, or provisions. The Saints in Utah contributed heavily toward bringing them to America and equipping the famous Handcart Expedition.

On June 9, 1856, the first of five companies started walking, the men and women pulling two-wheeled handcarts loaded with cherished belongings. Only infants and toddlers rode. Provisions were hauled in ox-drawn wagons, each adult being doled a daily ration of one pound of flour, a handful of coffee or tea, rice, and sugar. Eighteen cows provided milk, and hunters brought in some game, now scarce after a decade of heavy shooting.

The first few weeks brought severe muscle fatigue and blistered feet. Although the green lumber in the carts shrank in the July heat, the iron rims peeled from wheels, and the provisions proved far from adequate, the Saints averaged fifteen to twenty miles daily. They arrived in Salt Lake City on September 26 in surprisingly good shape for having walked across half a continent in three and a half months.

Two more companies arrived soon after, but the fourth and fifth walked into disaster. They started too late, dawdled, and fell afoul of October snowstorms. A desperate race from Salt Lake City with food, blankets, and mule teams arrived too late to save some 225 from death.

The Saints prospered, but Brigham Young's dream of keeping their kingdom of Deseret an independent state failed. In 1850 the Utah Territory was established. Only after eight more years of trouble, including skirmishes between Mormons and Federal troops, did Young finally accept the inevitable.

The pioneers in this painting are attempting to calm their horses as a prairie fire sweeps toward them. A man had to want something badly in order to risk his own life and the lives of his family on the Trail. At first, men went west for land; in 1849, the lure became gold.

COLLECTION OF CLAUDE J. RANNEY

10.
The Rush for Gold

One morning in January— it was a clear, cold morning— my eye was caught with the glimpse of something shining in the bottom of the ditch . . . I reached my hand down and picked it up; it made my heart thump, for I was certain it was gold."

Thus James Marshall described his discovery on January 24, 1848, of gold in the tailrace of a sawmill he had built for Captain John A. Sutter along the banks of the American River, in north-central California. The nugget, "half the size and of the shape of a pea," set off local excitement. From May 29 on, after the news was shouted in the Plaza at San Francisco, the word spread throughout the civilized world, initiating the greatest gold stampede in history.

"They say" stories abounded: "They say they're shoveling up the gold in sacks," or "they say the mountains in Californy are solid gold!" or "they say all a man needs to dig a fortune is a spoon and bucket!" No one described more picturesquely or briefly the headlong rush to California over the Oregon Trail than Appleton Harmon when he wrote, "We met a continual stream of Emegration for the mines runing meney of them half prepaird frantick and Crasey or distracted."

Easterners rushed for ship passage, Midwesterners for overland travel. Even before the ice went out of the Missouri River, young men on horseback were pouring into the river towns (mostly Independence, St. Joseph, and Council Bluffs), buying pack animals, and racing west. Steamboats unloaded thousands— along with their wagons, livestock, and supplies— at these towns. Here they swarmed, their stock milling and bawling aloud, until enough grass had sprouted on the plains to warrant their departure.

Some tried to reach California via the Santa Fe Trail and its connecting routes. Others cut across Texas and through New Mexico and Arizona. The Cherokee Trail opened from Fort Smith, Arkansas, crossed Oklahoma, followed the Arkansas River to Pueblo, Colorado, picked up the South Platte, and met the Oregon Trail traffic at Fort Bridger.

Those outfitting at St. Joseph rode due west and joined the Oregon Trail near present-day Marysville, Kansas. From Council Bluffs, most ferried the river and followed the Mormon Trail

Long after the great days of the Oregon Trail were past, stark symbols of the hardships faced by the pioneers remained. The old photograph above shows a wagon, its canvas stripped away by the wind, that had stuck in quicksand and been abandoned. The trailside graveyard below is a reminder of the epidemics that ravaged many wagon trains.

CHICAGO, BURLINGTON & QUINCY RAILROAD

Like most Americans, pioneers enjoyed having their pictures taken. They were often photographed on leaving home and again on reaching their destinations. This family poses proudly with its team and wagon in Nebraska in 1886.

MUSEUM OF NEW MEXICO

These women and children have set up camp in a peaceful grove, their hot and dusty day on the trail over. The boy in the foreground stands beside a saddle and harness; the other menfolk have probably gone off to graze the teams.

along the north bank of the Platte. But none of these routes carried as concentrated a stampede as the Oregon Trail. According to the St. Joseph *Adventure*, an estimated 20,000 persons in 2,850 wagons had crossed the Missouri by mid-May, 1849, with another 1,500 wagons rolling out from neighboring settlements.

In these jumping-off places the air was charged with excitement and thick with dust and flies. The din was terrific — the clang of hammers, axes being ground, oxen protesting their yokes; plus loud voices, mouth organs, fiddles and concertinas, and an occasional brass band. Over all wafted the aroma of baking bread and frying meat.

Pennants fluttered from wagon bows and ox yokes. Canvas tops sported brave slogans: "California or Bust!" or "Ho! the Diggings!" At Independence, whether buying or not, the men congregated around the mule market to dicker and swap the latest rumors. Riverbanks and meadows were jammed with wagons, many laden with merchandise to be sold for fantastic profit at the mines. The ground was littered with a large and weird assortment of mining machines, most of them useless. Vehicles ranged from wheelbarrows and handcarts to small and large wagons and iron boats on wheels.

Speed and greed set the tempo for 1849 and 1850. Patience, calmness, and consideration for the sick and injured, or for tiring animals, gave way to short tempers and selfishness. The earlier travelers had helped each other in

In 1849 a Washington draftsman named J. Goldsborough Bruff led a wagon train to California in search of gold and made these sketches on his way west. The view above shows the company relaxing near St. Joseph, Missouri. At left, a log bridge collapses under a wagon. Below, Bruff records the unhappy result of animals drinking at a polluted water hole in the desert.

125

THE HUNTINGTON LIBRARY

At Independence Rock, Bruff scratched his name on the unofficial "register" of the Oregon Trail, and then drew this panoramic view of the Trail winding along the Sweetwater.

many ways. Now, those who started out too heavily laden with flour, meal, or equipment, and were forced to lighten their loads, either spoiled or set fire to the discarded goods rather than help others to reach the gold fields.

Free from the gentling presence of families, the young men gambled, drank, grew beards, ignored soap, and were careless with guns. Paying no attention to the advice of plainsmen, they stocked up on pickles, crackers, peppers, sardines, sweets, and liquor. They endangered their lives with badly cooked food, polluted drinking water, and unsanitary habits.

A killer stalked the campgrounds and towns: Asiatic cholera. The dread epidemic had spread from Asia to Europe, and by 1832, to New Orleans, from whence it was carried upriver. Abating for a few years, it broke out fiercely again in 1847, following the Ohio and Mississippi river courses. By January, 1849, it had nearly devastated St. Louis, where some 6,000 died. Westbound emigrants fled the plague-ridden city, and being already infected, spread the disease through the Missouri river towns and out across the plains.

South of Independence, on the way up a modest ridge to the rolling prairie land, was Camp Cemetery, where many victims were buried. The actual Trail was lined with the graves of other unfortunates. As one Army officer wrote, "When we arose in the morning, it was a question among us as to who might fall a victim to it before another sun."

Many sober family men and homeseekers, women in silks and calico, girls clutching dolls, and boys shouldering stick guns walked daytimes and slept at night under the wagons with gamblers, thieves, and devil-may-care young adventurers. The gold rush swept along the best and worst of mankind. However, the first few weeks on the trail forced a communal discipline on even the laziest or most cantankerous. Before long, all realized that they must have some semblance of order and routine and share the labor and night guard duty if they hoped to reach California safely. Though there might be no established law west of Independence, each wagon company had its own laws, judge, and jury which dealt speedily with crimes and misdemeanors.

Judging from faded diaries and popular accounts of the forty-niners, this was also a high-spirited, singing stampede. One of their favorites was a parody on Stephen Foster's "O Susanna":

> Oh, California
> That's the land for me;
> I'm going to Sacramento
> With my washbowl on my knee.

The first joy of traveling past groves of leafy trees and man-cleared acres heightened as the wagons, staying on high ground, cut over vast fields of wild flowers. Nights were gay with dances, bonfires, singing, and card games. Gradually, however, the journey took its toll of strength and high spirits. Plains travel wore alike on rich man and poor, saint and scoundrel; and plains storms, the fiercest many had ever experienced, put the salty taste of fear in every man's mouth.

Beyond Fort Laramie the forty-niners met a small dilapidated pack train manned by grizzled trappers attired in stained buckskins and moccasins. This stubborn tag end of trappers and mountain men yielded the right of way grudgingly. Small wonder; for decades hadn't they been the lords of the Oregon Trail? And where would these dang newcomers and their useless truck be if the likes of Jed Smith, Jim Bridger, and old Tom Fitzpatrick hadn't opened the way? Like as not they'd be running around like chickens with their heads off if Jed and the Sublettes hadn't left a record of how to travel across the plains in companies, and survive. Greenhorns! *Wagh!*

Many years later the pioneers would write meandering reminiscences of the journey and almost always include an account of a horrendous Indian attack.

This charming picture of Fort Laramie was painted in 1866. It was then an elaborate Army installation, bearing little resemblance to the crude post of former days.

Actually, except for the earliest small trapper brigades, until after 1852 the Indians almost never attacked a road company. Harass, steal, stampede or kill livestock, pilfer, beg, and threaten — yes; massacre — no. The whites outnumbered them, and they were only passing through. Ranch houses, fences, and cattle herds were a later and greater threat to the Indians.

Inevitably the main flow of traffic spilled into side channels as the supply of grass, firewood, and game along the Trail was consumed by those caravans rolling in early May. Normally shallow fordings became impassable at floodtime, forcing the wagons to seek other crossings. Thus wagon tracks appeared as much as fifty miles from the original Trail, giving rise decades later to hot arguments and community rivalries as to just where the Oregon Trail ran.

Although the Platte bottom land seemingly could accommodate thousands, so small a thing as a spring drying up, or a grass fire, or polluted water, caused the wagons to thread new routes. Yet all these trails from Independence to Fort Hall were only offspring of the parent Trail, whose location from Independence (or St. Joseph) to Fort Laramie, over South Pass, and on to Soda Springs, Fort Hall, and the Columbia River was now well established.

Military authorities, recognizing the need for a chain of forts to protect the stampeders, purchased Fort Laramie from the American Fur Company for $4,000 and garrisoned it with officers and men from Company C, Mounted Rifles, and from Company G, Sixth Infantry. Travelers were still able to replenish their supplies at the commissary or sutler's stores, buy fresh oxen and mules, repair their wagons, register their parties, and mail letters back to the States. The winter of 1849-50 was mild, and the next summer the fort reeled under the impact of thousands upon thousands. By July, 37,570 men, 825 women, 1,126 children, and 9,101 wagons were entered in the fort's register.

Some would remember the trek to California as one long glorious picnic. Others, worn, dusty, and emaciated, would never cease to wonder how they survived, particularly over the dread portion after the turnoff from Fort Hall, across the desert and the Sierras to the mining towns. In one six-mile stretch in the Carson Valley, 2,000 wrecked wagons were counted after the 1850 rush. The whole distance, from Missouri to California, was known as "the trail of the moldering ox," referring to the thousands of oxen, mules, and horses that died on the way. The forty-niners had no time to bury their animals; they scarcely took time to bury their own dead deeply enough so wolves would not dig them up later.

Every single day great ingenuity, sacrifice, and courage were needed to infuse exhausted humans with enough energy to simply place one foot ahead of the other over plains, desert, and mountains until they finally reached the

Tension between Indians and pioneers grew during the gold rush. The Nez Perces in this 1855 water color are arriving at Fort Walla Walla for a peace conference.

golden land. A. C. Ferris vividly described some who arrived at the diggings in the fall of 1849: "The tired, starved, sick and discouraged travelers, with their bony and footsore cattle and teams. Men, women and children, and animals were in every state of distress and emaciation." Many, on arrival, were too exhausted to lift a shovel. They craved rest and a home, and California did fulfill its promise in many ways, if not with the rumored buckets of gold.

But not all the traffic flowed to California during the gold rush. Several hundred wagons pulverized the weeds and sagebrush sprouting each spring in the ruts of the Oregon Trail between Fort Hall and the Columbia.

Of his 1853 journey from Council Bluffs to Fort Walla Walla, Isaac Van Dorsey Mossman wrote of a terrible sandstorm, which "cut our hands and faces like knives," and after dark coyote concerts, "admission free." He went on to report, "We were often deluded by mirages, sometimes seeing ahead of us the most beautiful lakes . . . and when we imagined ourselves almost in reach of the water, the lake would disappear completely. This is no fairy tale...."

Although the gold fever abated somewhat in 1851, Mormon emigration quickened, and some 20,000 moved westward. Thanks to an Army-Indian treaty council in 1851 — one of the most spectacular pageants in American history, attended by whites, Sioux, Cheyennes, Arapahoes, Snakes, and Crows — the whites were granted permission to travel and to establish other forts along the Oregon Trail. Supposedly the treaty guaranteed a lasting peace, and in 1852 another 40,000 emigrants streamed by.

In 1853 and 1854 the gold fever was about over, and those emigrating were largely settlers with families. But on August 18, 1854, the rosy situation on the Trail erupted in a costly massacre. Some Brûle Sioux camped near Fort Laramie stole a cow from a Mormon, who reported the theft to the fort.

An arrogant young officer of the Sixth Infantry, Lt. John Grattan, marched out with twenty-eight soldiers,

Fast-riding Comanches brandishing lances attack a "circled-up" wagon train on its way to the California gold fields in 1849. This vivid drawing was done by Seth Eastman.

two cannon, and a drunken interpreter to arrest the culprit. Bitter words flared into a fight, and the entire military force was wiped out. The Indians then pillaged two other trading posts before fleeing the region. The other tribes abstained from violence, and so there was no further trouble that year or for most of 1855.

Meanwhile, Army authorities, well supplied with emigrants' exaggerated tales, decided the Brûlé Sioux must be punished. General W. S. Harney marched west from Fort Leavenworth with six hundred men. At Ash Hollow, 150 miles below Fort Laramie, they attacked Little Thunder's village, killing eighty-six Indians and capturing as many women and children. From that time on, the emigrants paid with their lives as the Sioux, and later other tribes, sought revenge until all were finally penned on reservations.

133

In the 1850's caravans of freight wagons began to rumble over the Oregon Trail. Delivering supplies to Army posts and mining camps was dangerous business; Frederic Remington's colorful painting of a supply train and its cavalry escort under Indian attack shows why.

11.
End of the Trail

With thousands providing their own transportation on the Oregon Trail, the business of freighting supplies along the route did not develop until the time of the gold rush. Then, as civilians demanded more protection from the Indians, and military posts were established, the question arose of how to forward supplies to them regularly and adequately.

In 1846 the Army attempted to provision General Stephen W. Kearney's force when it marched 1,000 miles west from Fort Leavenworth, following the outbreak of the war with Mexico. However, the inefficiency of the hired civilians, the inability of Army officers to handle this very specialized business, and the audacious Indian raids on the wagon trains resulted in a costly failure. The War Department ordered the quartermaster at Fort Leavenworth to contract with an experienced, professional freighter. He selected James Brown of Independence, who agreed to forward 200,000 pounds of supplies at eleven and three-quarter cents per pound to Santa Fe, and did so satisfactorily. Thereafter the Army used civilian freighters.

The next year, 1849, Brown took a partner, William Hepburn Russell, whose company had handled the first train of store goods transported between Westport and Santa Fe. Russell was of aristocratic background, moody and volatile. He avoided rough dress and speech and the arduous work of freighting, concentrating instead on the more genteel occupation of financing complex business operations.

The new firm, called Brown, Russell & Company, delivered 600,000 pounds of military supplies to Santa Fe under Brown's supervision. Unfortunately, before returning, Brown contracted typhoid and died.

Russell, William Bradford Waddell, a prosperous storekeeper, and an ex-teamster named Alexander Majors threw in together to gain a monopoly of government contracts for freighting across the plains. Waddell was cautious, conservative, and an expert purchasing agent. Majors was a sober, hard-working, religious man who made his bullwhackers sign a pledge promising not to use profane language, become intoxicated, mistreat the animals, or travel on Sunday. It was a commonsense pledge in such a hazardous

Having delivered their supplies, these mule-drawn freight wagons are returning eastward through the Colorado Rockies. Rock slides often blocked such mountainside roads.

DENVER PUBLIC LIBRARY WESTERN COLLECTION

business, and Majors soon had loyal family men working for him, leaving the rowdies to others.

The firm of Russell, Majors & Waddell operated out of Leavenworth, Kansas. Their 1,700 employees included wagon masters, stock tenders, cooks, laborers, clerks, blacksmiths, wheelwrights, carpenters, and messengers, one of whom was ten-year-old William F. Cody, the Buffalo Bill of later fame. By May, 1855, they had twenty trains on the road, each train consisting of twenty-six wagons.

Majors and the wagon masters superintended the highly important task of loading, since the slightest miscalculation could cause the cargo to shift or break away, delaying the train for hours. Once the loading was completed, the white covers secured, the wheels greased, and the spare timbers slung beneath the box, the bull teams were yoked on. Each wagon master received his bills of lading and a "train book," in which he entered his employees' names, the road purchases they made of tobacco and clothing, and pertinent road information.

Wagons and axles were made of seasoned white oak. The bottoms were curved slightly to prevent the loads

Raw new frontier towns depended on freighters and stagecoaches for everything from saloon mirrors to mail. Above, freight wagons circle up for a Denver photographer in 1866. At left, the citizens of Deadwood, South Dakota, watch the stage pull out.

from shifting when going up or down a hill. Wagon masters and stock tenders rode horses; bullwhackers walked on the left of the teams, cracking ten-foot whips over their heads. The oxen were yoked at daylight, and the train rolled until 10 A.M., laid over two or three hours, and then traveled until sunset. Heavy chains, wrapped in gunny sacks, were used to lock the wheels to prevent the wagons rolling out of control down steep slopes.

The "kitchen wagon" bulged with stick-to-the-ribs food: beans, corn meal, bacon, pickled pork, dried fruit, molasses, and coffee. The bullwhackers were divided into messes of five or six, with one serving as cook. Each man was assigned a rifle, a Colt six-shooter, and ammunition, and woe to the one who did not keep his arms in top condition. Majors rode out with the trains, cleaned his own plate, and slept on the ground. On Sundays he conducted simple services.

In June, 1857, the Army ordered the firm to transport 3,000,000 pounds of food and equipment to Utah to supply the soldiers dispatched to quell a Mormon uprising. Although the order came late, the job was carried through — but not without great loss to the firm. The Mormons burned off the grass so that there was insufficient feed for the oxen. They surrounded three of the trains, removed the supplies, drove off the teams, and burned the wagons. Blizzards further slowed the freighters, and only by superhuman effort did the other trains reach Utah.

During the summer of 1858, word spread of a big gold strike in the Pike's Peak region of what is now Colorado. Russell, Majors & Waddell foresaw a way to recoup their losses by monopolizing the freighting to the new diggings. They dispatched a large train to Denver the next spring and marketed the goods through a company store. They transported an additional 16,000,000 pounds, using 4,000 wagons, 40,000 oxen, and 5,000 men in an operation made unusually difficult by frontier hazards.

Meanwhile, Russell had decided to form a stagecoach company. Borrowing on the credit and reputation of the firm, but without consulting his partners, he and John S. Jones established the Leavenworth & Pike's Peak Express Company, which proposed to run regular service to Denver. The public hurrahed the idea, but sober businessmen thought Russell a reckless gambler. Majors and Waddell labeled his wild scheme financially unsound.

Russell went into debt heavily to purchase 1,000 mules and fifty Concord coaches. The important task of laying out the coach route and building way stations was assigned to Colonel William J. Preston of Leavenworth. A cheering crowd waved off the first two coaches departing from Leavenworth on April 18, 1859. Twenty bruising days later the ten passengers stepped out in Denver. History had been made, and Denverites were not the kind to contain their joy.

From the first, Russell lost money. He bought the contract to transport the United States mail between Missouri River towns and Salt Lake City. Russell's coaches rolled from Leavenworth and St. Joseph along portions of the Oregon Trail to Fort Kearney; along the south bank of the Platte to the forks; and along the South Platte to the Upper California Crossing, where there was now a way station named Julesburg. Here the Salt Lake-bound coaches crossed the South Platte, swung over South Pass, and took the Mormon route to Salt Lake City. The Denver coaches turned south to that mining camp. Way stations were spaced from sixteen to forty-three miles apart, and the one-way fare to Denver, exclusive of meals, was $125. The menu, at fifty cents to a dollar and a half a plate, included roasted chicken, butter, and fresh vegetables at eastern Kansas stops; wild turkey and antelope farther out; and finally plain ham and beans. Buffalo meat was a rare treat.

THE DAILY TIMES.

MONDAY MORNING, JANUARY 30, 1860.

LOCAL AND TERRITORIAL.

GREAT EXPRESS ENTERPRISE!

From Leavenworth to Sacramento in Ten Days!

Clear the Track and let the Pony Come Through!

In our telegraphic columns a few days ago, there was an item stating that it had been decided by the Government to start an Express from the Missouri river to California, and the time to be ten days; but we were no...

Enthusiastic announcements appeared in Western newspapers in 1860, signaling the start of the pony express. By the time the service was abandoned the next year, pony express riders had galloped 650,000 miles.

Once they could get supplies and mail, settlers reached farther out to the South Fork of the Platte. But Russell's stagecoach venture continued to lose money until Majors and Waddell agreed to purchase it and expanded operations under the name of the Central Overland California & Pike's Peak Express Company. Although in shaky financial condition, they poured more money into improving the service.

Considering the length of the route and the primitive conditions, the mail deliveries were surprisingly good. But not good enough, judging by a rising clamor from both Mormons and Californians. Finally, Congress appropriated enough money to tempt the nation's best express companies to bid for the business. The contract, guaranteeing $600,000 per year for six years of semiweekly mail service from the Mississippi to the Pacific, was awarded on September 6, 1857—not to Russell, Majors & Waddell, but to Butterfield & Company.

This company came into being when four experienced express agencies joined to break the monopoly of Pacific coast mail deliveries which had been long enjoyed by steamship companies. John Butterfield favored a southern route, rather than the Oregon Trail, to avoid winter storms. Dubbed the "Oxbow," it traced a great arc from Missouri through Texas, along the present-day United States-Mexico border, and northwest through California to San Francisco. The 2,800-mile journey was completed in twenty-five days.

Russell was outraged at the government's preference for the southern route. He felt his stagecoach company had proved the practicality of the shorter central route that included, for much of its length, the Oregon Trail. To prove his route was the better one, he hit upon a novel idea. On January 27, 1860, he telegraphed his son, "Have determined to establish a pony express to Sacramento, California... Time ten days."

WELLS FARGO BANK HISTORY ROOM

Two hundred and forty hours to travel 2,000 wilderness miles without escort? Scoffers considered it an impossible feat.

Majors and Waddell objected to underwriting a pony express because it could not possibly make money. Russell argued that it would bring "a world-wide reputation" to the company, and to the central route, and thus influence the public and Congress that their express company should receive a fat contract. This, of course, would solve the firm's financial difficulties.

The history of the pony express was spectacular, dramatic, and brief. Westbound mail was made up in New York and reached St. Joseph by railroad. On April 3, 1860, as a crowd cheered, a band blared, and a cannon boomed, a slight, red-shirted rider leaped into the saddle and raced off. A similar episode took place in San Francisco. Each rode some thirty to fifty miles, during which time three horses were used, and two minutes were allowed for each change-over. West of Salt Lake City, on April 8, the relay riders pounded past each other, while still others completed the ride at both ends on schedule.

The feat electrified the nation and gained for Russell, Majors & Waddell the "world-wide reputation" Russell wanted. It also gave American folklore a romantic chapter second to none, and wherever the flying hoofbeats touched the old road, it brought added glory to the Oregon Trail. In some 150 round trips the pony express did much

Stagecoaches reached into every corner of the West. This handsome lithograph, made about 1860, shows a coach on a Pacific coast run. Mt. Shasta is in the background.

to keep the Far West informed of events leading to the outbreak of the Civil War and helped mobilize sympathy for the Union cause.

In 1861 Congress appropriated a million dollars per year for the overland mail service. This included the pony express until it was terminated after the completion of the overland telegraph line on October 24 of that year. The pony express' blaze of glory lasted only about eighteen months.

The Butterfield Company received the lush 1861 contract, but it formed a working arrangement whereby Russell, Majors & Waddell's stagecoaches handled the Missouri River-Salt Lake City run, and Butterfield's coaches took the run through Nevada and California. But even this business could not stave off disaster for the pioneering firm. They had incurred too heavy an indebtedness and went bankrupt. Their chief creditor, Ben Holladay, who had cut his teeth stagecoaching in Colorado, bought the equipment on March 21, 1862, at public auction.

Holladay's Overland Stage Line meant new fame for the Trail. Atchison, Kansas, was the starting point; the next major stops were Marysville, Fort Kearney, and Julesburg. Because of constant Indian trouble along the Sweetwater River, Holladay abandoned the South Pass road and moved his coaches up the South Platte, intercepted the Cherokee Trail opened by the forty-niners, and followed it to Fort Bridger. This portion soon became known as the Overland Trail. Beyond the fort, the coaches stopped

In an attempt to keep the memory of the Oregon Trail alive, Ezra Meeker traveled it by wagon from west to east in 1906. He is seen here ready to leave Pendleton, Oregon.

at Salt Lake City and Placerville, California.

In time Indian raids caused Holladay losses amounting to some $375,000. He could see the handwriting on the wall. Already the transcontinental railroad had reached a point across the Platte from Fort Kearney. Holladay sold out to Wells, Fargo & Company, which continued running coaches to Denver and Salt Lake City.

With the driving of the golden spike that joined the two halves of the transcontinental railroad in 1869, the Atlantic and Pacific were linked with ribbons of steel. The wilderness was forever spanned, and a nation united.

The railroad did not bring an immediate end to covered wagon travel. Wagons were still toiling up the Oregon Trail and crossing South Pass as late as 1895. But the trail blazing and dangers were all behind these latter-day travelers. There were towns and villages, supply stations and ranches, all along the way now. Often these last wagons had to detour because the worn ruts were erased by plows or blocked by barbed-wire fences. The Indians, corralled on their reservations, were no longer troublesome.

Of the thousands upon thousands who traveled the historic highway, only Ezra Meeker carried on a campaign to save the old Trail from complete obliteration. In 1852, when he was twenty-one, he had come west by ox team to Oregon. When he was seventy-five, in 1906, he hitched up a small wagon and team and retraced the Trail eastward, stopping at every hamlet to urge people to raise markers commemorating the Oregon Trail. Not satisfied with the response to his idea, he made the trip by ox team and wagon again in 1910, by automobile in 1915, and by airplane in 1924. Only on isolated stretches of the plains or along the rocky ground of the Sweetwater could he see remnants of this great and glorious road.

Robert Stuart and Jedediah Smith, Tom Fitzpatrick and Captain Bonneville, the Whitmans and Jesse Applegate and Brigham Young—they assaulted the stern wilderness so the unknowns could be mapped and a nation unified by the greatest settlement road in American history, the Oregon Trail. With courage and perseverance and unflagging optimism, they made a conquest seldom equaled by great armies and military leaders. Within their lifetimes, game trails became wagon trails over mountain passes and plains; and moccasins gave way to hooves, and hooves to wooden wheels, and wheels to iron rails and oiled highways. Like a mighty artery, the Oregon Trail pumped strength and untold wealth into the fledgling nation rushing headlong to maturity and world stature, and it remains today the greatest symbol of America's westering.

OVERLEAF: *By 1872, when Samuel Colman painted* Ships of the Plains, *the days of these giant freight wagons were numbered. The saga of the Oregon Trail was about over. Today nothing remains but a few wheel ruts.*
UNION LEAGUE CLUB OF NEW YORK

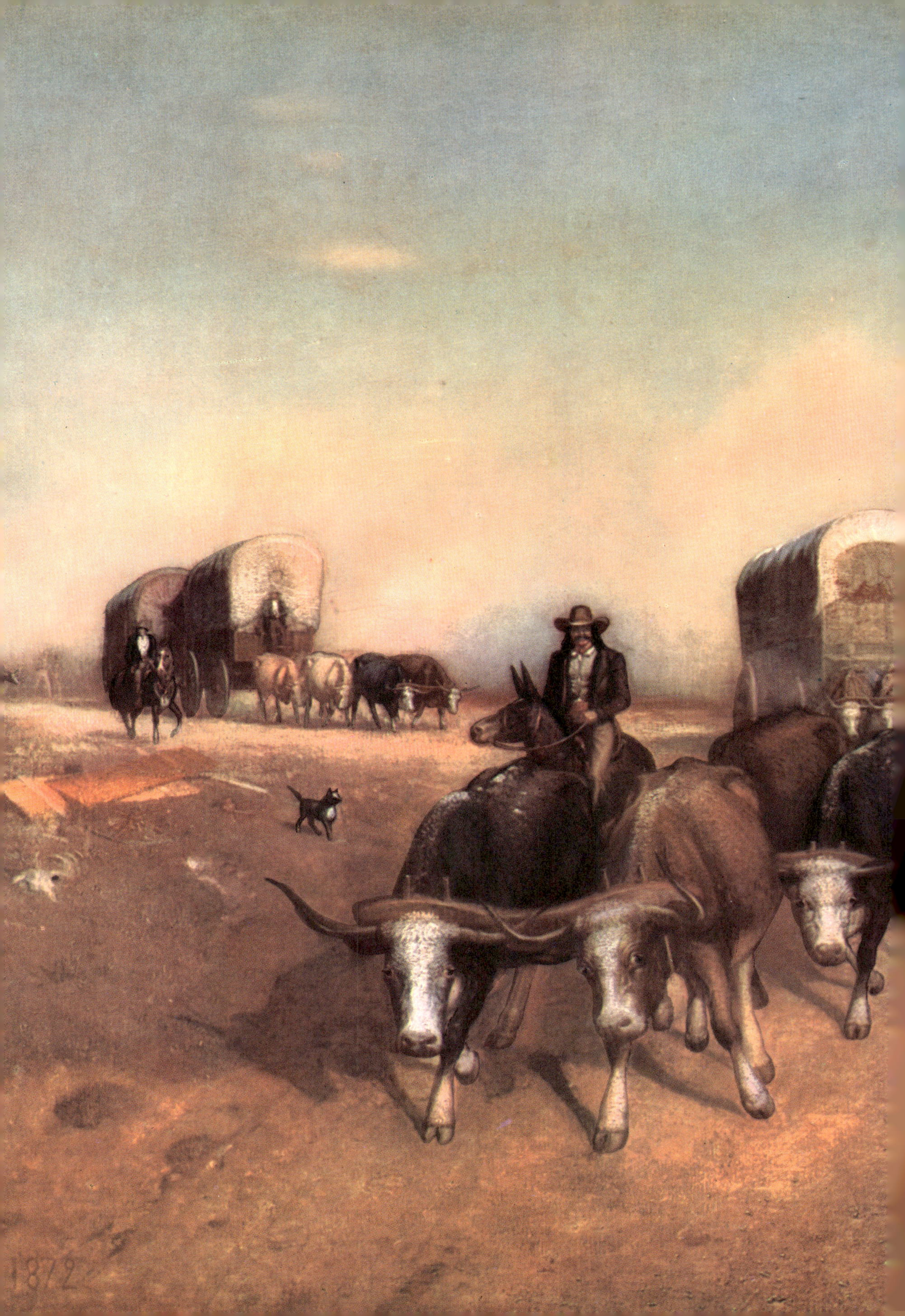
1872

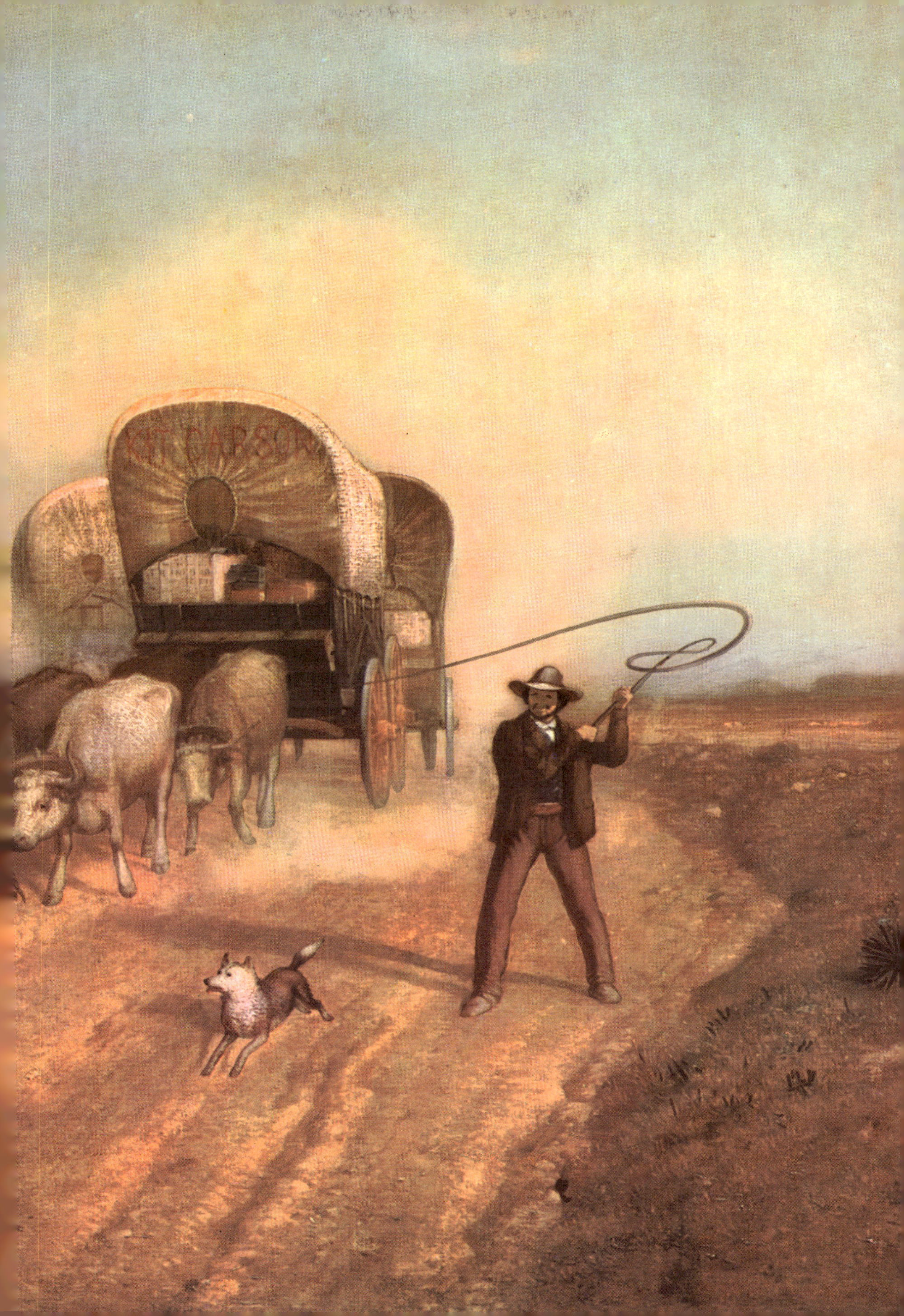
KIT CARSON

AMERICAN HERITAGE PUBLISHING CO., INC.

BOOK DIVISION

Editor
Richard M. Ketchum

———— ∗ ————

JUNIOR LIBRARY

Editor
Stephen W. Sears

Art Director
Emma Landau

Assistant Editors John Ratti · Mary Lee Settle

Picture Researchers Julia B. Potts, Chief
Dennis A. Dinan · Mary Leverty

Copy Editor Patricia Cooper

ACKNOWLEDGMENTS

The Editors wish to thank the following individuals and organizations for their assistance and for making available pictorial material in their collections:

American Pioneer Trails Association, New York City — Howard R. Driggs
Denver Public Library — Mrs. Alys Freeze
Gilcrease Institute of American History and Art, Tulsa, Okla. — Dean Krakel
Huntington Library, San Marino, Calif. — Robert O. Dougan
Knoedler Galleries, New York City — William Davidson, Elizabeth Clare
Missouri Historical Society, St. Louis — Mrs. Ruth K. Field
National Broadcasting Company, Project Twenty — Daniel W. Jones
Oregon Historical Society, Portland — Thomas Vaughan
Claude J. Ranney, Malvern, Pa.
University of Wyoming Library, Laramie — Gene M. Gressley
Walters Art Gallery, Baltimore — Edward S. King
Yale University Library, New Haven — Archibald Hanna

The sketch on pages 78-79 is reproduced by permission of Mrs. Emily Blackmore and the Book Club of California.

FOR FURTHER READING

Allen, Eleanor. *Canvas Caravans.* Binfords & Mort, 1946.
Andrist, Ralph. *The California Gold Rush.* American Heritage Junior Library, 1961.
Applegate, Jesse. *A Day with the Cow Column.* Chicago University Press, 1934.
Apsler, Alfred. *Northwest Pioneer: the story of Louis Fleischner.* Farrar Straus & Cudahy, 1960.
Beard, John W. *Saddles East: Over the Old Oregon Trail.* Binfords & Mort, 1949.
Botkin, B.A. (editor). *A Treasury of Western Folklore.* Crown, 1951.
Burt, Struthers. *Powder River.* Farrar & Rinehart, 1938.
*Callahan, Lorna. *Where the Trail Divides.* McGraw-Hill, 1957.
Coons, Frederica B. *Trail to Oregon.* Binfords & Mort, 1954.
Daugherty, James. *Marcus and Narcissa Whitman: Pioneers of Oregon.* Viking, 1953.
De Voto, Bernard. *Across the Wide Missouri.* Houghton Mifflin, 1947.
De Voto, Bernard. *Course of Empire.* Houghton Mifflin, 1952.
*Hough, Emerson. *The Covered Wagon.* Grosset & Dunlap, 1922.
Irving, Washington. *The Adventures of Captain Bonneville.* Binfords & Mort, 1954.
*Fiction

Jones, Evan. *Trappers and Mountain Men.* American Heritage Junior Library, 1961.
*Lathrop, West. *Keep the Wagons Rolling.* Random House, 1949.
Miller, Helen M. *Benjamin Bonneville.* Messner, 1957.
Mirsky, Jeannette. *The Westward Crossings.* Knopf, 1946.
Monaghan, Jay. *The Overland Trail.* Bobbs-Merrill, 1947.
Morgan, Dale L. *Jedediah Smith and the Opening of the West.* Bobbs-Merrill, 1953.
Morgan, Dale L. *The Great Salt Lake.* Bobbs-Merrill, 1947.
*Morrow, Honoré. *On to Oregon.* William Morrow, 1946.
Lavender, David. *Land of Giants.* Doubleday, 1958.
Parkman, Francis. *The Oregon Trail.* Doubleday, 1959.
*Steele, William O. *We Were On the Oregon Trail.* Grosset, 1956.
West, Ray B., Jr. *Kingdom of the Saints: The Story of Brigham Young and the Mormons.* Viking, 1957.
Wibberly, Leonard. *Zebulon Pike: Soldier and Explorer.* Funk & Wagnalls, 1961.
Winther, Oscar Osburn. *Via Western Express & Stagecoach.* Stanford University Press, 1945.

Index

Bold face indicates pages on which illustrations appear

A

Adventures of Captain Bonneville, The (Irving), 53
American Fur Company, 53, 130
American River, 74, 120
Applegate, Jesse, 89, 91
Army-Indian Treaty Council of 1851, 132
Ashley, General William H., 37, 39, 42, 45
Astor, John Jacob, **29,** 30, 45
Astoria, **31,** 32, 33, 42, 45, **78-79**
Astorians, 32, 37, 58

B

Bartleson, John, 101
Bear Meadows, 92
Bear River, 92, 103
Beaver, 19, 28, 30, 37, 39, 45, 53, 59, 98
Beer Springs, 92
Benton, Senator Thomas Hart, 111
Bidwell, John, 99, 101, 103
Bidwell-Bartleson Expedition, 99, 101, 103
Bierstadt, Albert, paintings by, **80-81, 84-85**
Big Sandy Creek, 39
Big Sandy River, 19
Blue Mountains, 22, 92

Blue River, 19
Boise River, 59
Bonneville, Captain Benjamin Louis Eulalie de, 48, 49, **49,** 53, 62, 98
Bridger, Jim, 37, **43,** 59, 64, 98, 113, 129
Brown, James, 136
Brown, Russell & Co., 136
Bruff, J. G., drawings by, **4-5, 124-125, 126-127**
Buffalo, 19, **24-25,** 26, 51, 91, 101, 112
Burnett, Peter, 89
Butterfield, John, 141, 144
Butterfield & Co., 141, 144

C

California, 22, 96, 98, 99, 103, 120, 130, 131. *See also* Gold Rush
California Trail, 16-17 (map), 22
Camp Cemetery, 128
Carson, Kit, 59, 64, 98, 111
Carson Sink, 103, 104
Carson Valley, 130
Carver, Jonathan, 28
Catlin, George, 65, painting by, **65**
Central California & Pike's Peak Express Co., 141

Cerré, Michael, 48
Cherokee Trail, 16-17 (map), 120, 144
Chimney Rock, **15**, 19, 51
Cholera, 62, 64, 128
Christian Advocate and Journal, 58, 62
Church of Jesus Christ of Latter-Day Saints, *see* Mormons
Clark, William, **27**, 28, 30, 32, 58
Clayton, William, 112, 113
Clyman, James, 37, 39, 104
"Coasts of Nebraska," 19, 49
Colorado River, 98
Columbia, 27, 28
Columbia River, 12, 22, 27, 28, 30, 92, 130, 131
Congress, U.S., 45, 79, 107, 141, 144
Continental Divide, 19, 28, 39, 53
Cook, Captain James, 28
Cottonwood Spring, 90
Council Bluffs, Iowa, 120
Court House Rock, 19

D

Dalles, The, 22, **23**, 92
Denver, Colo., 140
Devil's Gate, 19
Donner Lake, 105
Donner-Reed Party, 103-106

E

Eastman, Seth, painting by, **135**
Elm Grove, Mo., 78, 86
Emigration, 106, 117, 130, 132. *See also* Gold Rush, Great Emigration of 1843, Mormons, Pioneers

F

Farnham, Thomas Jefferson, 76, 77, 101
Fitzpatrick, Thomas, 37, 39, 59, 64, 67, 70, 82, 98, 101, 129
Fontenelle, Lucien, 62, 64
Forts
    Atkinson, 45
    Boise, 22, 59, 62, 71
    Bridger, 71, 113, 144
    Hall, 19, 22, 59, 78, 92, 106, 130
    Kearney, 144
    Laramie, **14**, 19, 67, 91, **129**, 130
    Leavenworth, 45, 136
    Osage, 48
    Walla Walla, 22, 62, 71, 92
Forty-niners, *see* Gold Rush
Frémont, Lt. John Charles, 110, 111, 113
Fur Trade, 28-31, 39, 42, 45, 46, 48, 53, 59, 78. *See also* Trappers

G

Gold Rush of 1849, 74, 118, 120, 124, 128-132
Goodyear, Miles, 67
Gratton, Lt. John, 132
Gray, Captain Robert, **27**, 28
"Great American Desert," 36
Great Britain, 30, 45, 53, 106
Great Emigration of 1843, 12, 84, 86, 89-92, 106
Great Salt Lake, 98, 116
Great Salt Lake Valley, 103, 104, 108, 111, 116
Greeley, Horace, 83
Green River, 42, 53, 64, 91
Green River Valley, 19
Greenwood, Caleb, 103
Grey, William, 74, 83

H

Handcart Brigade, **114-115,** 117
Hastings, Lansford, 82
Hastings' Cutoff, 104
Henry, Andrew, 37, 42
Holladay, Ben, 144, 145
Holladay's Overland Stage Line, 144
Hudson's Bay Company, 30, 42, 59, 76
Humboldt River, 98, 103, 104
Hunt, Wilson Price, 32

I

Independence, Mo., 12, 22, 45, 86, 120, 124, 130
Independence Rock, 19, 70, 91, 126
Indians, **18,** 26, 27, 32, 33, **50,** 58, **63,** 64, 67, 70, 71, 98, 106, 129, 130, 132, 133, 136, **back endsheet**
    Blackfoot, 32
    Brûlé Sioux, 132, 133

Cayuse, 71, 105-107
Cheyenne, 91, 101
Chinook, **56-57,** 58, 59, 62
Comanche, 98, **132-133**
Crow, 33, 39, 51
Flathead, 58, 59, 64, **68-69,** 101
Kansas, 86
Kiowa, **36-37**
Nez Perce, 58, 59, 64, 71, **131**
Osage, 86
Shoshone, 32

J

Jackson, David E., 44, 45
Jackson, William H., pictures by, **44, 88, 96-97**
Jefferson, President Thomas, 26, 42
Julesburg, Colo., 140

K

Kansas River, 19, 42, 48
Kelley, Hall Jackson, 58, 62
Kelsey, Mrs. Benjamin, 101, 103

L

Lane, General Joseph, 107
Lapwai Mission, 71, 83
Leavenworth, Kans., 140
Leavenworth & Pike's Peak Express Co., 140
Lee, Daniel, 58, 59, 74
Lee, Jason, 58, 59, 62, 64, 70, 74-76, 79, 106
Lewis, Meriwether, **27,** 28, 30, 32
Lewis and Clark Expedition, 27, 28, 30, 32, 58
Liberty, Mo., 62
Little Blue River, 42
Little Sandy River, 19
Long, Major Stephen H., 36

M

Mail, U.S., transportation of, 140-142, 144
McDougall, Duncan, 32
Mackenzie, Alexander, 30
McLoughlin, John, 71
Majors, Alexander, 136, 138-142
Marshall, James, 120
Marysville, Kans., 144

Meek, Joe, 74-75, 78, 107
Meeker, Ezra, **144,** 145
Miller, Alfred Jacob, paintings by, **front endsheet, 13, 14-15, 20-21, 40-41, 43, 46-47, 50, 52, 54-55**
Mission Boards, 62, 64, 74, 75, 83
Missionaries, 56, 58, 59, 62, 64, 67, 70, 71, 74
   Catholic, 67, 69
   Congregational, 62, 74, 106
   Presbyterian, 58, 62, 74, 106
   Methodist, 58, 62, 70, 74, 106
   See also Lee, Spalding, Whitman
Missions, 62, 64, **70,** 79, 82. *See also* Lapwai Waiilatpu
Mississippi River, 26, 128
Missouri River, 12, 28, 30, 32, 33, 37, 42, 45, 65, 124
Mormon Trail, 16-17 (map), 112, 120, 140
Mormons, 108, 110-117, **114-115,** 140
Mules, 49, 51, 86, **100**

N

North Platte River, 19, 33, 49, 91, 113
North West Company, 30
Nutall, Thomas, 59, 62

O

Old Spanish Trail, 16-17 (map)
Oregon country, 12, 22, 27-30, 45, 74, 76, 77, 86, 98, 99, 103, 106, 107, 131
Oregon Dragoons, 76, 77, 101
"Oregon question," 53, 74, 106
Oregon Trail, route of, 12, 16-17 (map), 19, 22, 130
Oregon Trail, The (Parkman), 106
Otter, 28, 30
Overland Trail, 16-17 (map), 144
Oxbow Route, 16-17 (map), 141
Oxen, 13, 48, **88,** 103, 140

P

Pacific Fur Company, 30
Panic of 1837, 75, 86
Parker, Reverend Samuel, 62, 64, 70, 71
Parkman, Francis, 106
Pike, Lt. Zebulon M., 36
Pioneers, 6, **7,** 10, 12, 17, 19, 22, **87, 88,**

94-95, 118-119, 120, 122-123. *See also* Emigration, Gold Rush, Mormons
Pittman, Anna, **75**
Platte River, 13, 19, 42, 49, 90, 91, 112
Point, Father Nicholas, painting by, **68-69**
Polk, President James, 106
Pony express, 141, 142, 144
Pratt, Orson, 113, 116
"Protestant Ladder," **67,** 68

R

Railroad, transcontinental, 145
Remington, Frederic, paintings by, **93, 134-135**
"River of the West," 28
Robidoux Brothers, 99
Rocky Mountains, 19, 37, 45, 51
Russell, Majors & Waddell, 138, 140, 142, 144
Russell, William Hepburn, 136, 140-142

S

Sagebrush, 19, 71, 78, 91, 103
St. Joseph, Mo., 120, 130
St. Louis, Mo., 28, 32, 33, 42, 45, 128
Salt Lake City, Utah, 116, 117, 145
San Joaquin Valley, Calif., 98, 103
Santa Fe Trail, 16-17 (map), 42, 86, 98, 120
Schallenberger, Moses, 104
Scott's Bluff, **15,** 19, 51
Seymour, Samuel, painting by, **36-37**
Sierra Nevada Mountains, 22, 98, 103, 105
Smith, Asa, 74, 75, 83
Smith, Hyrum, 110, 111
Smith, Jackson & Sublette Co., **44,** 45
Smith, Jedediah, 37, **38,** 39, 42, 44, 45, 71, 98, 99, 129
Smith, Joseph, 110, **111,** 116
Snake River, 19, 22, 30, 32, 42, 59, 71
Soda Springs, 19, 92, 98, 106, 130
South Pass, 19, 33, 39, 45, 53, 70, 144, 145
South Platte River, 19, 91, 144
Spalding, Eliza, 64, 65, 67, 70, 71
Spalding, Reverend Henry Harmon, 64, 65, 67, 71, 74, 83
Stagecoaches, **138,** 140-145, **142-143**
Steamboat Springs, 19, 92
Steamboats, 45, **65,** 141
Stevens, Elisha, 103, **103**
Stevens-Townsend-Murphy Party, 103-104

Stewart, Captain William Drummond, 15, 59, 64, 67
Stuart, Robert, 32, 33, **33**
Sublette, William, 45
Sutter, Captain John Augustus, 74, 120
Sweetwater River, 19, 33, 39, 42, 51, 95, **126-127,** 144

T

Tamahas (Cayuse Indian), **105**
Tonquin, **30-31,** 32
Townsend, John Kirk, 59, 62
Trappers, 20, 21, 31, **34-35, 40-41,** 53, **90, 99,** 129. *See also* Fur Trade
Trappers' Rendezvous, 45, 59, **60-61,** 70, 74, 98
Truckee Meadows, 104

W

Waddell, William Bradford, 136, 140-142
Wagons, **10-11,** 12, 18, 42, **44,** 45-49, **46-47,** 53, 71, **72-73, 84-85,** 86, 93, 100, 103, 112, 113, 121, **124-125, 133**
  Dearborn Carriage, **44,** 45
  Freight, 128, 134-140, **134-135, 137, 139, 146-147**
  Red River Cart, 101
Waiilatpu Mission, 71, 74-78, **76-77,** 83, 92
Walker, Joel, 77, 78
Walker, Joseph Reddeford, 48, **52,** 77, 98
Wells, Fargo Co., 145
Western Emigration Society, 99, 101
Whitman, Dr. Marcus, 62, 64, 65, 67, 70, 71, 74, 75, 77, 78, **82,** 83, 86, 89, 91, 92, 105-107, **107**
Whitman, Narcissa Prentiss, 65, 67, 70, 71, 75, 77, 83, 107, **107**
White, Dr. Elijah, 79, 82, 83
Willamette River, 22, 62, 92
Willamette Valley, 6, 74, 92
Wind River, 39
Wind River Mountains, **20-21,** 33, 39, 45, 53
Wyeth, Nathaniel J., 58, 59, 62

Y

Yellowstone, **65**
Yosemite Valley, 98
Young, Brigham, 108, 110-113, **113,** 116, 117

153

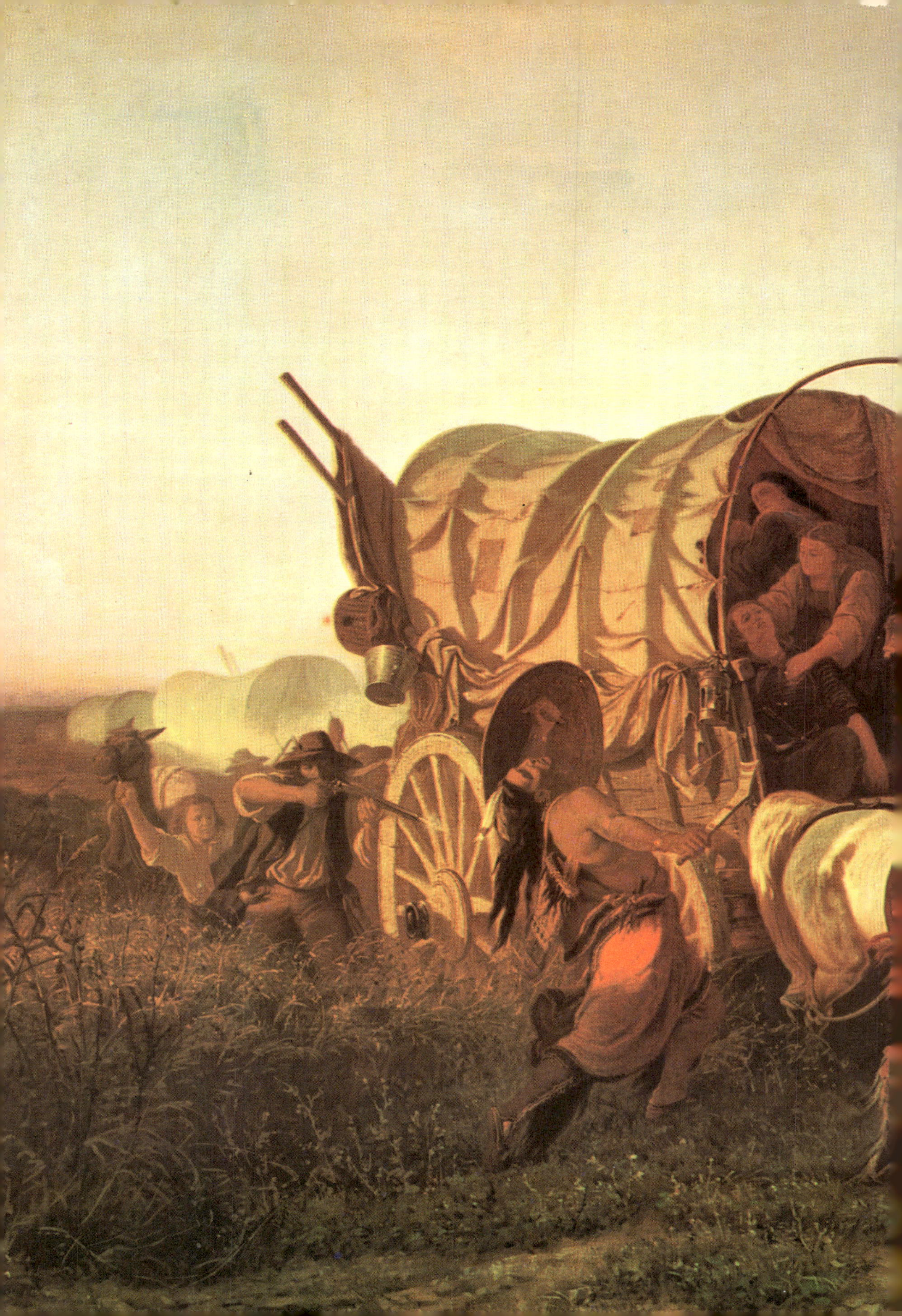